maker.

maker.

Wild

Published in 2020 by Welbeck
An imprint of Welbeck Publishing Group
20 Mortimer Street
London W1T 3JW

A CIP catalogue record for this book is available from the British Library
ISBN 978 1 78739 398 1

Printed in Dubai
10 9 8 7 6 5 4 3 2 1

maker.

Mike Warren

Wild

15 Step-by-step Projects for the Great Outdoors

WELBECK

maker.

Wild

Contents

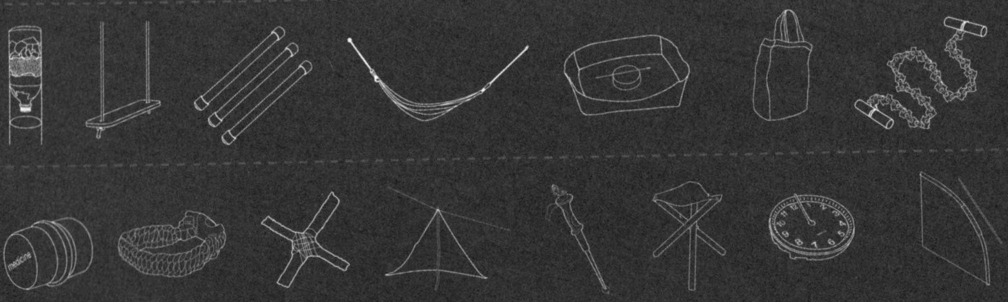

Introduction

Being out in the wilderness doesn't have to mean a long camping adventure: it can be something as simple as an afternoon hike in the woods. The adventure just means stepping away from civilization and returning to nature, something most humans crave.

It's a chance to recharge the mind and take a break from the endless screens we look at all day. This book aims to reconnect you with nature by exploring some projects to make in the wild, or which can be taken with you to make your day in the woods a little more interesting.

Trekking out into the wilderness is exciting but needs to be approached with care: you don't want to get lost or hurt during your adventure. The wilds can be unforgiving, though there are a few things you can make and do to make your life easier. Being resourceful is key when far away from civilization – and being prepared is even better. In this book I hope to provide ideas that are both inventive and clever, and which you can take with you as you venture into the wild, as well as a few projects that are just for fun.

In this book I've tried to make the materials used applicable to more than one project. That way, you don't need to buy too much and carry it with you. Some projects assume you're already in the wilderness and will need to make do with whatever you can find. An unpleasant reality of the modern age is that rubbish has managed to find its way into even the most remote areas. With this in mind, a few projects reuse old plastic bottles, or rope that you may come across on your adventures. I encourage you to make do with what you have around your home to make these projects, or be inspired and remix them in your own way. Even though this book is for entertainment, the resourcefulness required for wilderness survival can come in handy, both at home and in the great outdoors.

Happy making!

Mike Warren, 2020

Project 01. Water filter

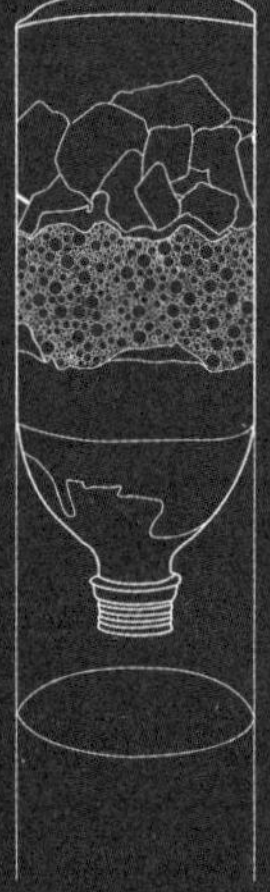

Water, shelter, fire: this is the survival triangle. We talk about shelter and fire elsewhere in this book, and here we'll talk about water. You may find yourself near a water source, but can we make it safer to drink? We can mitigate some of the concerns by using a water filter. In an unexpected situation, this could save your life.

Tools & Materials

Tools:

- Knife
- Scissors

Materials:

- Charcoal
- Sand
- Gravel
- 2 soda bottles
- Cloth
- Kindling

Step 1: Charcoal

Charcoal is a critical ingredient for making a water filter. In a controlled setting, charcoal is made by burning wood and then starving the fire of oxygen. This method works by heating the organic compounds in the wood without burning, leaving behind the black lumps we all recognize.

If you have the time and expertise to make an airtight chamber, burn wood, seal the container airtight, and wait for the charcoal to cool, then please do! For the thirsty survivalist, the next best thing is to use what you have on hand – probably charcoal from last night's fire.

Step 2: Finding the right charcoal

Even with the remains of a large fire, we can't use just any coals we find. We're looking for large lumps of featherweight charcoal with no organic material or unburned sections left.

You'll know you have the right stuff if you can see deep cracks in the charcoal, and if it breaks apart in clean chunks in your hands.

Step 3:
Grind charcoal

To make the charcoal an effective filtering agent, we need to increase its surface area. To do that we'll grind up the charcoal into smaller pieces, allowing water to access as much of the charcoal as possible when it's in the filter.

Find a large flat rock to use as a grinding surface, then use a small rock to grind the lumps of charcoal into a rough powder.

Step 4: Gather filtering media

Charcoal is the most critical ingredient in our water filter, but not the only one. In order to trap some of the larger bits that may be floating in the water from our source, we need media of different sizes. For our filter media we'll use sand, fine gravel and medium gravel. This graduated approach ensures that larger material is caught while travelling downwards through the smaller media, which catch progressively smaller material until we reach the final layer of charcoal - which will remove microscopic elements in the water.

Step 5: Cut bottles

To capture the filtered water, and hold the filtration system, we need two plastic bottles, ideally the same size. Cut the top off one bottle, and the bottom off the other, using the point where the bottles change diameter as your cut line.

Step 6: Cut cloth

To keep the filtration media separated, and prevent it from spilling out, you will need to place cloth sections between the media. Using one of the cut bottles as a guide, cut circles of cloth that match the diameter of the soda bottle. Cut as many circles as the number of filtration media you're using; for example, four filtration media will need four cloth circles.

Step 7: Layer filtration media

Use the bottle without a bottom as the filtration section. Turn the bottle so that the cut end is facing upwards, then lay a cloth circle in the narrow neck of the bottle. This cloth will prevent the filtering media from spilling out. Keep the bottle cap on to seal the bottom of the filter.

Gently place the crushed charcoal into the bottle on top of the cloth at the narrow end of the bottle, then place another cloth circle over the charcoal. Continue adding media, from fine to coarse, placing a cloth circle between each.

Step 8:
Set filter into the capture receptacle

Set the filter into the second bottle with the top cut off. If you're using the same type of bottle, the two should nest nicely.

Step 9:
Fill with water

Fill the filter with water, letting the water saturate the media. Unscrew the cap and place the filter bottle into the capture bottle.

Step 10:
Wait

The water needs time to pass through the filter and out the bottom. If you have more bottles you can make a few filters and increase production.

Step 11: Science and warning

The various media are filtering out the large and small particulate matter from the water, turning it into cleaner water. Of course, this does assume the filtration media is itself clean. To that end, all media should be washed to remove any foreign materials or dirt. Since, however, you will be washing in an unknown water source, the next step is to spread the media into a very thin layer on a rock and allow direct exposure to sunlight. This will sterilize the media as best you can before use in a filter.

Charcoal is an effective filter because it's very porous, trapping contaminants. However, the charcoal used in this project is not pure, and charcoal filters are effective when they have maximum time in contact with water.

So, while this filter does work, and is a great demonstration of filtering water in the wild, this method should be used only in an emergency. To take extra precaution with your drinking water, boil it on the campfire before drinking any water found in the wild.

Mini project
Fire starters

Tools:

- Lighter, or heat gun

Materials:

- Wax candle
- Cotton pads

Few things are more essential when in the wilderness than fire. Making fire reliably, and quickly, is something every outdoor adventurer should know how to do. Luckily, this is made easy with these simple fire starters, enabling you to make a roaring fire on your first try.

Step 1:
Gather supplies

Any wax candle will do to make fire starters, and a wax candle should already be part of your survival gear. A longer candle will, however, be easier to hold while it is lit. For making the starters, I used cosmetic cotton pads, but any natural material will work. You could substitute cloth, or even moss if you're desperate.

Step 2: Melt wax

Ignite the candle and carefully drip the wax onto the cotton pads. Take the time to completely saturate the pads. Let the wax cool completely before handling or storing the pads.

Step 3: Store rounds

Once the wax has cooled, the pads will be hard, allowing them to be stacked up neatly and stored in an airtight container until ready for use.

Step 4: Usage

For best results, use one to two fire starters in a nest of dry kindling. This will ensure the fire catches and starts igniting the kindling.

Step 5: Light starter

Ignite one of the starters and wait for it to catch, then slowly lower the starter into the kindling nest to start the fire. Add more twigs as necessary to build your fire.

Project 02. Tree swing

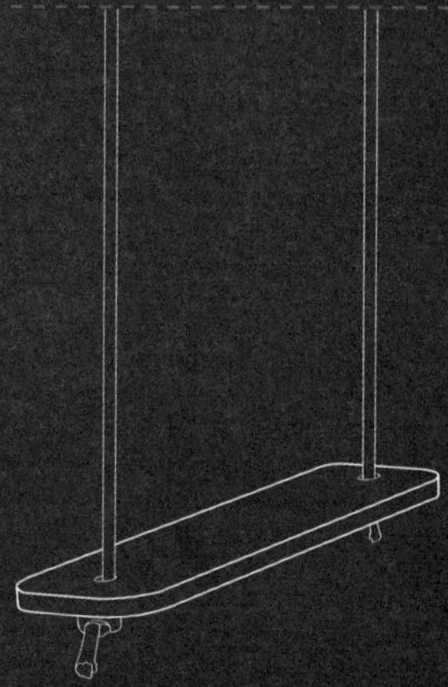

Few things are more carefree than a swing, especially combined with the serene tranquillity of nature. Though there are many ways to make a swing, I like this method as it's easily removable and doesn't damage the tree.

Tools & Materials

Tools:

- Drill
- Saw
- Knife
- Lighter
- Tape measure
- Level
- Sandpaper

Materials:

- Scrap wood plank
- Approximately 15 m (50 ft) rope cut in 2 equal lengths
- Approximately 1 m (3 ft) chain cut in 2 equal lengths
- Chain shackles
- Large washers

Step 1: Materials

It's important to only use materials that have a load rating, which should be conspicuously displayed on the package. The sizing of the shackles, chain, rope, washers, and drill bit will depend on what you find in your local hardware store. Every item should have a load rating which should be much higher than the expected weight on your swing. The rope I used is rated for 270 kg (600 lbs) which is the weight of three grown adults, much heavier than this project needs. This is the lowest load-rated item on my list: the chain and shackles are rated much higher.

Spend the time to find the right chain and rope first. Then, look for shackles that are large enough to fit two links of chain as well as washers that have an opening that matches the diameter of the rope you're using. The drill bit used to create the seat opening should also match your rope diameter.

Step 2: Round seat corners

Rounding off the corners of the swing seat gives a much nicer appearance, and prevents any injuries from being hit with a sharp corner mid-swing. However, if you prefer a more rustic look skip the next two steps.

Use a paint can lined up with a corner to create a smooth curve. Mark that curve with a pencil, repeating the process for each corner.

Step 3:
Cut edges

Use a saw to cut away the curved corners of the swing seat. If you want to create a sweeping corner, use a coping saw or a bandsaw. This too is optional – cutting away the sharp corner is all that's needed.

Step 4:
Smooth edges

Smooth down the edges of the seat, which will feel much nicer to sit on than a sharp edge. Also sand the cut corners to smooth out any rough edge left from the cut.

Step 5: Drill seat openings

Use a drill bit that is the same size diameter as the rope. It doesn't need to be exact, since the rope can be rolled and squished through a slightly smaller hole, and a slightly larger opening won't affect performance.

Starting on the top of the seat drill about 38 mm (1.5 in) from each end of the seat. Drill completely through the swing seat.

Step 6:
Sand openings

Sand both rope openings on the swing seat. This will ease the sharp corners and prevent premature wearing of the rope.

Step 7: Seal or paint

Seal the wood with a protective coat of polyurethane. This will help keep it from deteriorating when in the elements and will prevent the swing from being damaged by weather over the years.

Step 8: Find branch

Locate a branch that you'd like to attach your swing to. The branch should be on a healthy tree, thick enough to support your weight, and located close to the trunk of the tree to prevent too much movement when under load. If you've brought your swing into the wild without a ladder then consider a tree that is also climbable.

Drape the chains over the selected tree branch about 1 m (3 ft) apart.

Step 9: Tie rope eye

Take one end of the rope and double back about 40 cm (16 in). Tie a simple knot using the doubled up rope end to create an eye. Leaving the other end untied. Repeat with the second rope section.

Step 10: Singeing rope ends

Synthetic rope is great not only because it's inexpensive, but after cutting to length you can easily stop it from fraying or unravelling by using a flame to melt the end.

Gently rotate the cut end of the rope over the flame from a lighter or candle to melt the cut end. Keep the end of the rope in the flame until the entire end catches and you can see all the loose fibres of the cut end melted and sealed up in a molten blob. Blow out the flame and hang the rope with the cut side facing downward for about a minute until the plastic has cooled.

Step 11: Attach shackles

Use the shackles to join the chain ends together and which will then hold the rope eye.

Shackles are designed for this purpose, easing the transition from rope to chain, so find shackles that are large enough to accommodate the rope diameter and both ends of the chain.

Step 12: Attach rope eye

Feed one of the rope eyes into a shackle, then reattach the shackle to one of the chains. Allow the loose end of the rope to fall to the ground, then repeat the process on the other shackle.

With both shackles tight on the chain and the rope securely in the shackles, the hard part is over. Climb down from the tree or ladder and set up the swing seat.

Step 13: Attach swing seat

Push the loose rope ends through the drilled seat openings. From the underside of the swing, put a large washer on each rope end. These washers will help keep the rope from coming up through the seat after it's been tied.

Step 14:
Measure

Move the swing seat to the desired height, taking into account that there will be some sag when under load. Measure off both sides to get roughly the same distance from the ground.

Step 15:
Tie knot

Tie a simple knot on the loose end of the rope underneath the swing seat, capturing the washer between the tied knot and the underside of the swing seat. Do not tie this knot tightly as we'll need to fine tune the seat before we're finished.

Step 16:
level

Use a spirit level to level out the seat, creating a steady surface to swing on.

Step 17:
Cut excess rope

When you're satisfied with the height of the swing, tighten the knots under the seat and use a sharp knife to cut the excess rope. Use a flame to seal the cut rope ends to stop fraying.

Project 03. Polar bear tubes

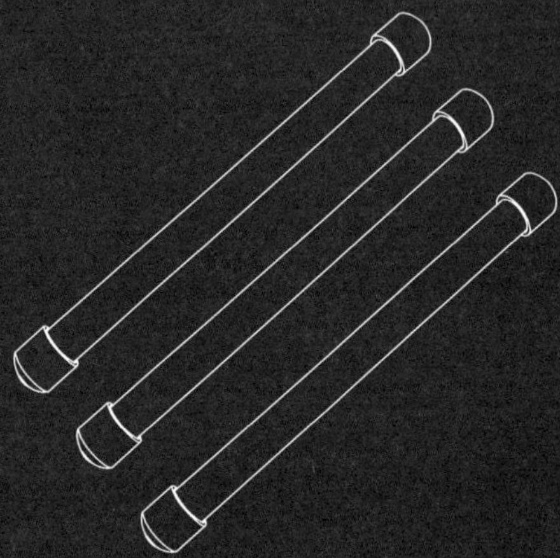

Keep your foodstuffs nicely chilled for hours with custom-made reusable ice tubes. These are a little different than regular ice packs: their tubular shape offers a long surface area to maximize the cooling area. Since they are custom-made, you can make these tubes in any length you need, short or long.

Tools & Materials

Tools:

- Tape measure
- Hacksaw
- Sandpaper
- PVC cement
- Marker

Materials:

- PVC tubes, at least 25 mm (1 in) diameter
- PVC caps, matching diameter

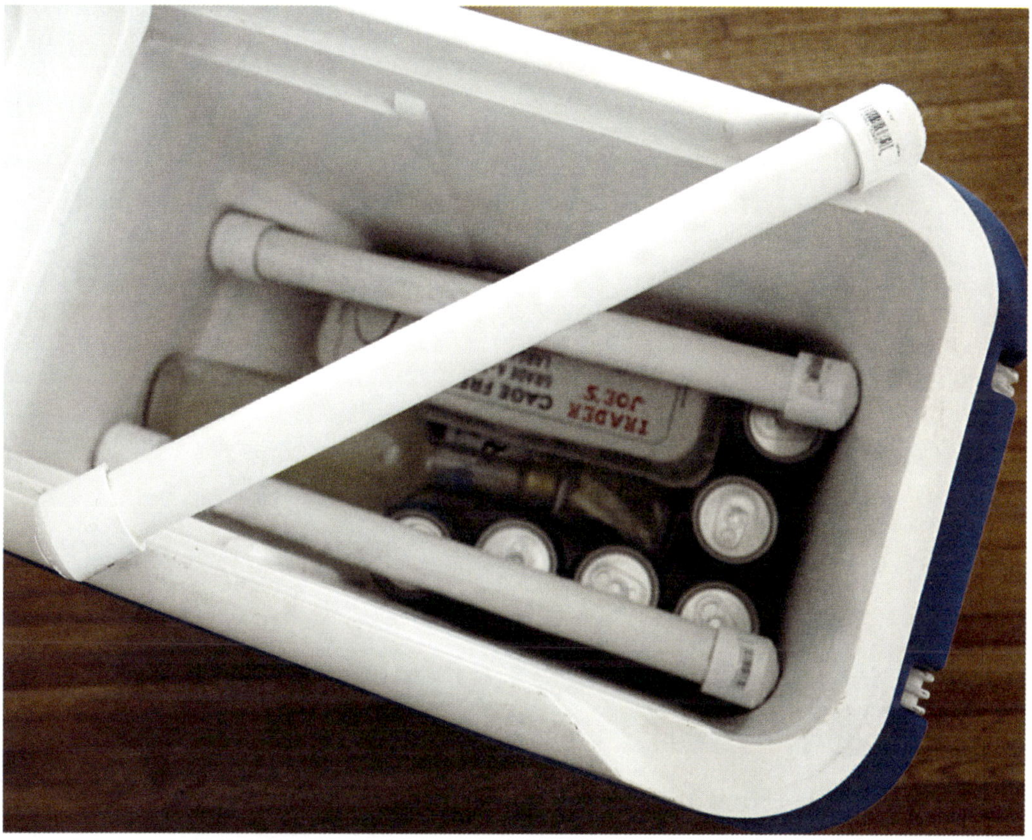

Step 1:
Measure length

Measure the length of the interior of the cooler. You'll need to make the length of the tubes about 50 mm (2 in) shorter than the measured length, to account for the caps that will go on the PVC tubes afterwards.

These tubes can be made from any diameter PVC tubing, but should be at least 25 mm (1 in) in diameter so that there is enough volume inside to keep the tubes cool for a few hours. Obviously, larger diameter tubes will stay cooler than small diameter tubes.

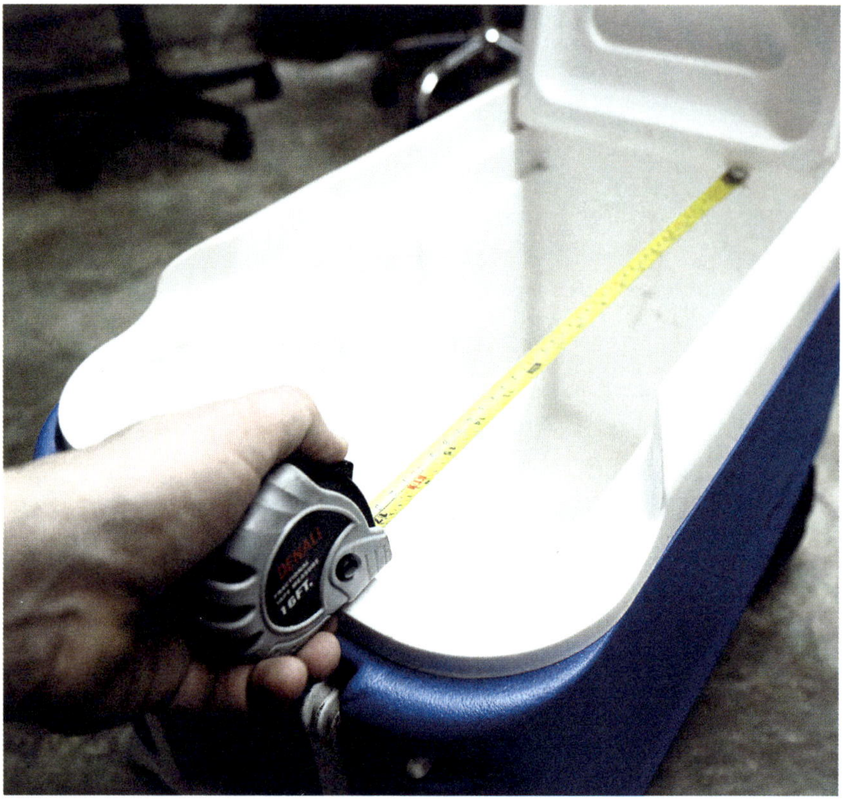

Step 2:
Make cuts

Clamp the PVC tube securely and make a cut at your mark using a hacksaw. A hacksaw is a good choice for cutting PVC, as the teeth of the blade are very small and make a neat cut. A larger tooth blade such as a wood saw would leave the ends very jagged.

Step 3:
Clean ends

Whenever you cut PVC, there will be burrs on the end, which will need to be cleaned off. Most times these burrs can be removed with your fingers. However, if you want a nice smooth finish on the edge use a fine grit sandpaper to gently rub around the cut ends.

Step 4:
PVC glue

To secure the PVC caps to the tubes, a special type of adhesive is needed: PVC cement.

This cement is different from regular glue. Instead of relying on an adhesive bond like regular glue, PVC cement creates a chemical reaction with the PVC, which welds the two pieces together. This makes the PVC watertight and able to withstand some amount of pressure.

Step 5:
Attach caps to one tube end

Using the in-cap applicator, smear PVC cement onto one end of a PVC tube, then quickly press and turn a PVC cap onto the cemented end. Since the cement is a chemical reaction, you will need to work quickly before the cement dries.

While pushing the cap onto the cemented tube end, add a twisting motion to ensure that the cement is evenly applied to both surfaces during connection.

Step 6: One end for each tube

Continue cementing a PVC cap on one end of each PVC tube, leaving the other end open to fill with water later.

The cement will take only moments to bond the caps to the tubes, but excess cement may be tacky for a few minutes after pressing the caps on. It's best to let the cement dry for 10 minutes before filling with water. Clean up any excess or squeezed-out glue with a damp cloth.

Step 7: Find water fill line

Before filling each tube with water, we need to find the fill line. The tubes can't be filled completely, otherwise they would explode when the water inside expands while freezing.

We can make a fill line by measuring approximately three-quarters of the tube and making a mark.

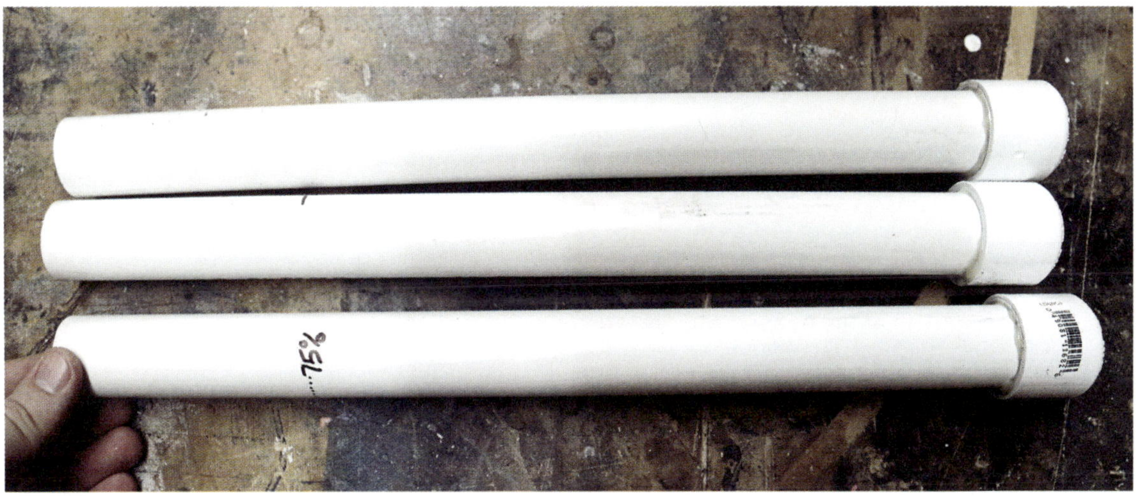

Why the gap?

When frozen, water expands by about 9 per cent of its volume. The gap gives us plenty of room to allow for water expansion.

Step 8: Fill tubes

Fill the tubes with tap water up to the fill line.

Step 9:
Cap tubes

Cap the open end of the tube used for filling with a smear of PVC cement around the tube and then press on the PVC cap.

Step 10:
Freeze tubes

Once capped, the tubes can go into the freezer overnight. Alternatively, keep a few in there all the time so you're always ready to keep things cool.

Step 11: Keep cool

These reusable tubes are great for keeping your cooler extra cold, and in a way that keeps the cooling evenly distributed along the food. The best thing about polar bear tubes is that they don't leak and won't make all your food wet like ice does when it melts.

Food for thought

When packing food for the wild, consider food that requires as little packaging as possible. Or better still – pack food in materials you can use for later survival projects.

Project

04.

Easy hammock

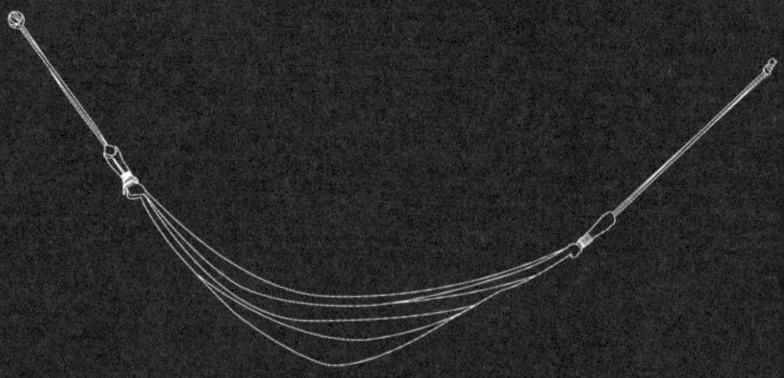

Increase your ability to relax with nature by making the easiest hammock with just a few simple materials. The great thing about this project is that you can substitute almost any foldable sheet to make a hammock, like a tarp or the fly from your tent. The hardest part of this project might just be finding two trees to string your hammock between!

Tools & Materials

Tools:

- None!

Materials:

- Bedsheet
- Paracord
- Rope
- 2 trees

Step 1: Open sheet

Open your bedsheet completely to assess the dimensions. Ideally, the longest side of your sheet should be longer than you are tall, though this project still works if it is a little smaller.

Step 2:
Fold in half

Find the short side and then fold your sheet in half along it. You'll want to double up the sheet to ensure it can hold your weight when you lie on it.

Step 3:
Gather sheet ends

Continue folding your sheet along the short edge until the sheet is about 150 mm (6 in) wide. The entire fold doesn't need to be neat, just the ends of the sheet which will be tied up.

Step 4:
Fold end over

Gather one end of the folded sheet and fold over approximately 300 mm (12 in) from the end.

Step 5:
Tie end

Using paracord, bind the folded end of the sheet, leaving an opening where rope can be passed. Make sure to wrap the ends tightly with enough paracord to prevent the sheet from coming loose – I used about 10 turns. Tie off to secure the binding with a double knot. It doesn't matter what type of knot you use as long as it's secure.

Step 6: Pass rope through sheet opening

Take a section of rope and fold it in half, making a loop in the middle of the rope. Pass the middle rounded end of the rope through the opening of the folded sheet, creating a loop about 150 mm (6 in).

Step 7: Loop rope

Pass the loose ends of the rope through the looped opening that was passed through the bound sheet.

Step 8: Cinch rope

Pull the rope tight, cinching the rope down on the bound end of the sheet. This will be what secures the hammock to the tree.

Repeat steps 3 to 8 on the other end of the sheet to complete the hammock construction.

Step 9: Tie hammock to tree

To tie your hammock up, find two suitably distanced trees and wrap one end of the hammock rope around a tree at about chest height.

To secure the rope, pass the loose end of rope under the hammock end of the rope and then make a knot, pulling tight to secure the knot as close to the tree as possible.

Step 10:
Tie second knot

A second knot will secure the first and prevent the rope from untying. To tie the second knot, pass the loose end of the rope over the hammock end and then under and through the opening.

Pull the rope tight. Repeat the knot process on the other end of the hammock, securing it to the tree.

Step 11:
Open sheet

With the hammock secured to the tree, gently open the sheet to reveal the seating area. The easiest way to get into the hammock is to straddle the hammock with a leg on each side, then sit into the middle of it.

Now kick your feet up and relax!

Project
05.
Duct tape compass

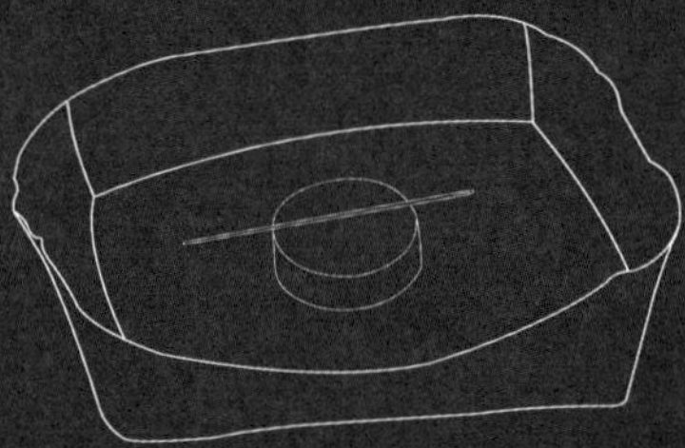

When packing, it might seem trivial to try and optimize the weight of a small compass. Not only is this compass foldable and compact, but it shows that you can make one from almost anything. For that day when you're lost without a compass, here's a great way to improvise and find your way home.

Tools & Materials

Tools:

- Knife
- Magnet
- Scissors

Materials:

- Duct tape
- Cork
- Needle
- Magnet

Step 1: Lay out first layer of duct tape

Lay out 3–4 strips of duct tape, sticky side up, overlapping each strip to form a small sheet of duct tape. Lay a second layer of duct tape on top of this sheet, sticky side down, creating a duct tape sheet with the sticky layer sandwiched inside.

Step 2:
Cup duct tape sheet

The duct tape sheet needs to be cupped in order to hold water. To make this easier, I placed the square bottom of another container in the middle of the duct tape sheet and pulled the sides up against the container. Any container will work, and if you're careful you may not need to use one at all.

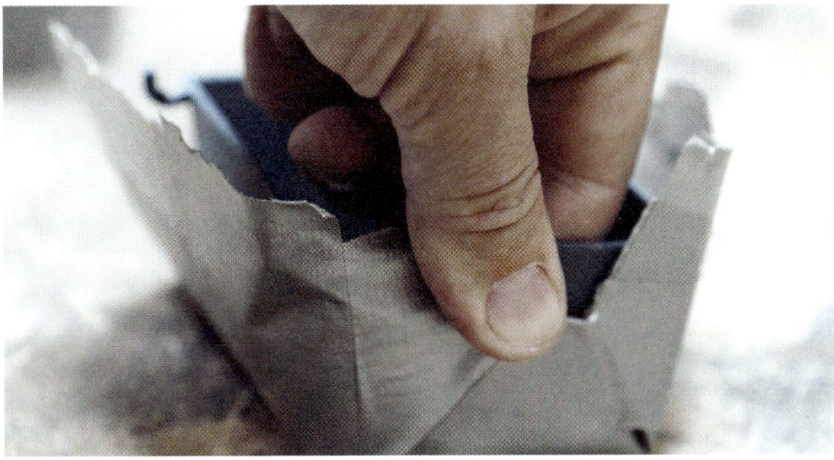

Tip:

If you're in the wild without a container to shape your duct tape around, don't be afraid to use a flat stone or piece of wood.

Step 3: Tape edges

Once the duct tape sheet has a cupped shape, use a small amount of duct tape to seal the edges and corners together to retain the shape, and ensure the cupped duct tape you just made will hold water without leaking.

Step 4: Trim top edge (optional)

The top edge of your duct tape compass may be ragged from when it was created. This can easily be cleaned up by trimming away the top of the cupped duct tape shape to make a level top.

Set this aside for now while we work on the float.

Step 5: Cut cork platform

In order to get accurate directions, there needs to be a platform that will float in the cupped duct tape vessel, upon which the needle will rest.

Cut a 12 mm (½ in) slice from a wine cork. We'll use this as our floating platform for the needle to rest on.

Step 6: Magnetize needle

In order to get the needle to point north/south, it first needs to be magnetized. To do this we can stroke a magnet along the length of the needle *in one direction only*, imbuing the needle with slightly magnetic properties.

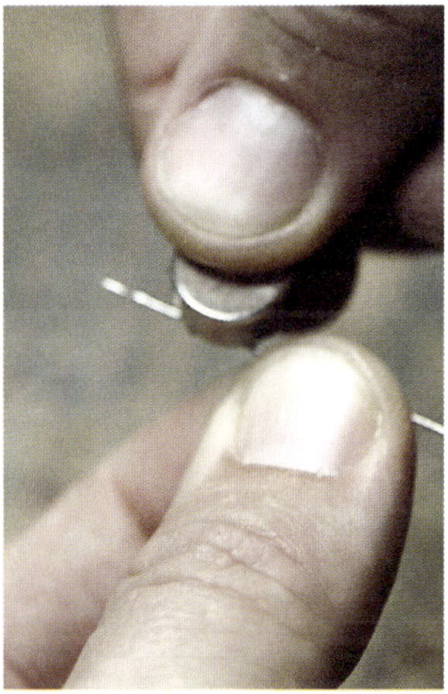

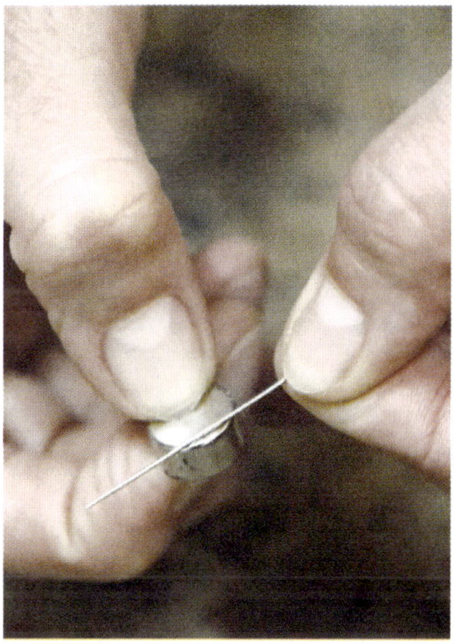

Step 7: Assemble and orientate

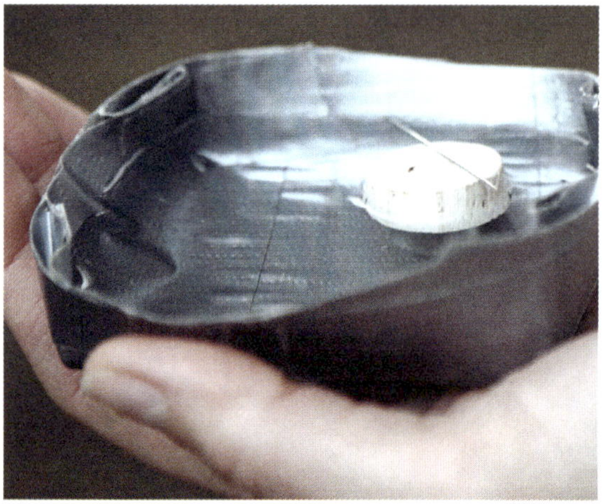

Fill the duct tape cup about halfway with water. Place the magnetized needle on the cork slice and then place both into the water gently. Once magnetized, the needle will point towards the strongest magnetic pole relative to your location: north in the northern hemisphere and south in the southern hemisphere.

From this initial bearing, you can determine the remaining cardinal bearings by drawing an imaginary line perpendicular to the needle bearing. Remember, this information orients you based on magnetic poles, not geographic poles.

This project neatly demonstrates the principle of orientation using household items, and it might even help you to find your way home one day!

Tip:
Stuck for duct tape? Use any still body of water, like your drinking flask, a puddle or the bottom of a discarded plastic bottle.

Project 06. Waterproof clothing & kit

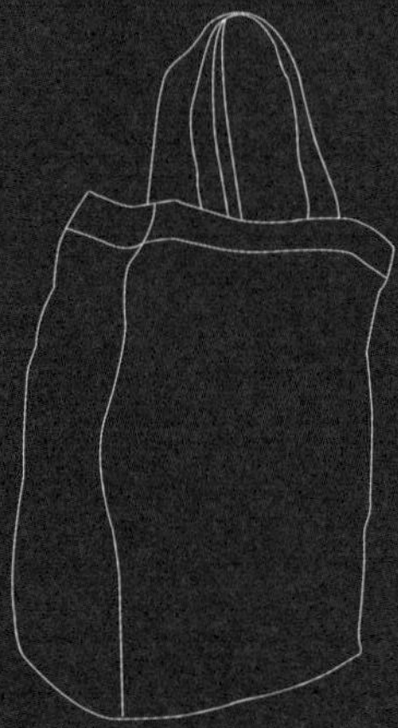

Most shop-bought waterproofs are expensive, and often ineffective. My version gives me entire control of the waterproofing process. Using brushes over an aerosol, I can ensure full coverage on all my gear. This inexpensive and flexible solution is a great way to make almost anything waterproof.

Tools & Materials

Tools:

- Paintbrush
- Disposable mixing cup
- Stirring stick
- Caulking gun

Materials:

- Mineral spirits/white spirit/solvent naptha
- 100 per cent clear silicone caulking

Step 1: Source materials

Pure silicone caulking will be labelled "100 per cent pure". Always look for "silicone I" caulking as it doesn't have any additives like mould-retarding agents; we want pure silicone. To thin the silicone, we will use mineral spirits, white spirits, or solvent naptha. You can find all these materials at your local hardware store.

Step 2: Pour materials

Using a disposable container, squeeze in a sizable blob of silicone caulking, then mix in mineral spirits. A rough ratio is four parts mineral spirits to one part silicone. Mix thoroughly with a stir stick, spending time to ensure a consistent mix. Expect to be mixing for at least two minutes to ensure that the mineral spirits have fully been incorporated.

Step 3: Check consistency

Although this method will work even if it's not fully mixed, you can end up with blobby clumps when it's applied, or thin areas that aren't as waterproof. The mix should be watery, easily dripping off the brush when lifted from the container.

Step 4:
Application

In even strokes, brush the mix onto your garment. The goal is to have the mix penetrate the material – but not completely soak it.

Step 5:
Hang dry

After application, the mineral spirits will need to evaporate, allowing the caulking to dry before the garment can be worn or the kit used. Leave the item hanging overnight to dry completely.

Step 6:
Get wet

Once it's dry, you're ready to get into the wild and get messy. The waterproofing should last at least a season, but areas with lots of stitching or areas that crumple may need touch-ups after a while.

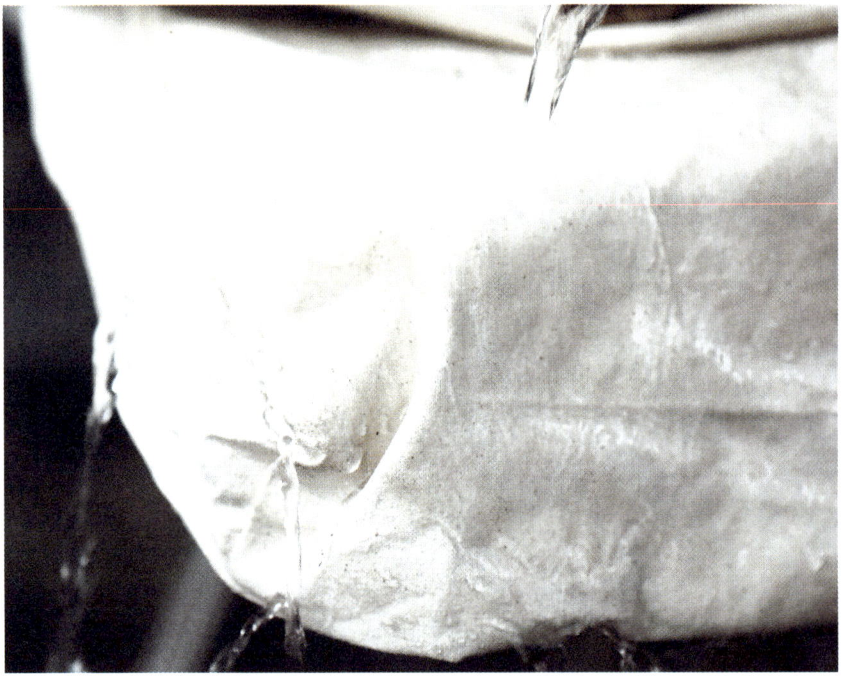

Project 07. Foldable saw

Who knows when a chainsaw might play a part in your adventure? Whether your chainsaw has run out of juice, or the chain has slipped, there's still a way to use what you have to take down some trees. Here we'll repurpose an old chainsaw chain into a collapsible saw, easy to use and ready for the next trunk takedown.

Tools & Materials

Tools:

- Hacksaw or rotary tool
- Wire snips

Materials:

- Stiff wire
- Chainsaw chain
- Sticks or dowels

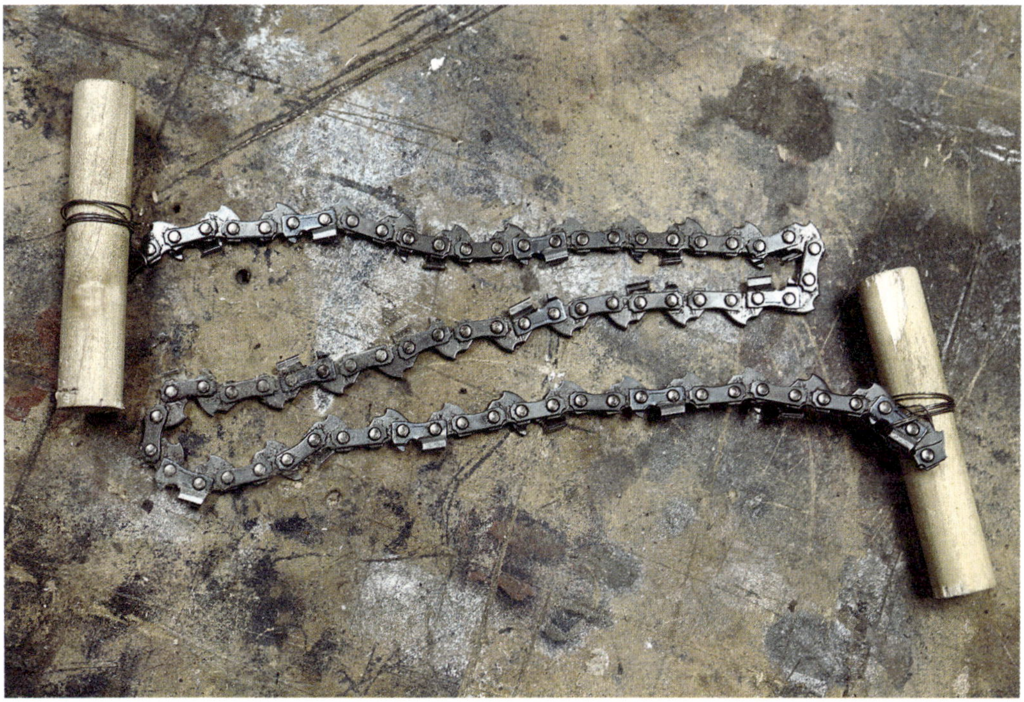

Step 1:
Sever chain circuit

A chainsaw chain is a linked circuit, much like a bicycle chain. To modify the chain for our needs, we'll need to break the circuit and have one long chain. If your chainsaw chain is already broken, skip this step.

If you're out in the wild, you'll need to use a hacksaw to break the chain; but if you're in the workshop, you can use a rotary tool with a cutting wheel to sever the chain circuit.

Tip:
Find a linkage with a single rivet or connecting piece; this will be the easiest place to attack to sever the chain circuit.

Step 2:
Shorten chain

If your chainsaw has a long bar, the chain could be unmanageable. This will need to be cut down in order to be used as a folding handheld saw. You will want a chain segment about as long as your arm.

Find a single connecting link on the chain approximately an arm's length from one end and make the cut to shorten the chain.

Step 3:
Handles

Since we can't hold onto the chain with our bare hands, we'll need to make handles on each end. I've used wood dowels cut down to about 15 cm (6 in) long, but branches would also work fine if you're in the wild.

Step 4: Feed wire through chain ends

With the stiff wire on the spool, feed about 60 cm (24 in) of stiff wire through the end linkage at the end of the chain. Holding on to the stiff wire at the chain, pull the spool back until it matches the length (60 cm/24 in) that was fed through.

Step 5:
Wrap chain ends

Now cut the wire and wrap it around the centre of the dowels tightly, securing the chain end to the dowels. Make sure to feed the wire ends through the end linkage a few times for a good connection.

Repeat this process on the other handle.

Step 6: How to use

Chainsaw chains have teeth on only one side of the chain, so make sure the toothed side is facing towards you while cutting. Approach the tree you want cut down and eyeball a spot on the trunk that will be easy to work the saw at – I like about chest height.

Place the saw on the backside of the tree and hold on to each handle, ensuring the teeth of the chain are facing you. Chainsaw teeth are directional, so will cut effectively in only one direction. It's best to have the teeth pointing towards your dominant hand, allowing your stronger arm to do the pulling required to make a cut.

Gently start by working the chain back and forth along the back side of the tree until you've started cutting a groove into the wood. Increase the force on the pull stroke to cut away material. When pulling the chain back in the other direction, make sure to not pull into the cut: you want the chain to skip easily out of the cut groove so you can reset for the cutting stroke.

This tool can easily take the place of a conventional wood saw in your backpack at a fraction of the volume. Something to consider the next time your chainsaw breaks down and you've got a fire to build.

Project 08. Waterproof container

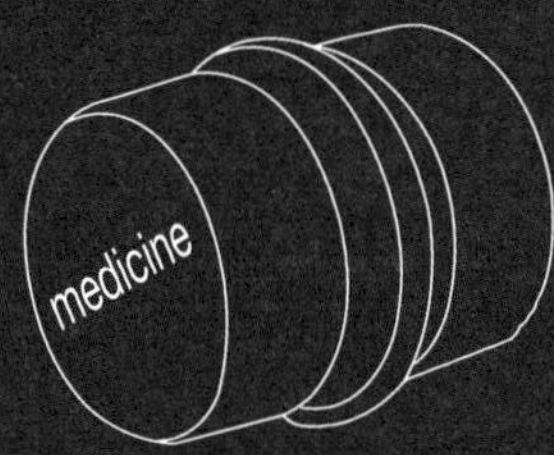

On a trek, both the size and weight of items in your pack are important. Smaller items, such as medicine or spices, can make for a big impact when combined together. Compact your pack and downsize your small gear into these waterproof containers that take up minimal space.

Tools & Materials

Tools:

- Knife/scissors

Materials:

- Plastic bottles
- Glue
- Sticky labels

Step 1:
Source bottles

Plastic bottles are great for this project because they are ubiquitous and inherently waterproof – it's also a great way to reuse and recycle single-use plastic. Source two identical bottles for each container. Making sure that the bottles are the same size helps when fusing the two sides together. While it is possible to make a container with dissimilar bottles, the best results will be from identical bottles. Both bottles will also need to have caps.

Step 2:
Remove excess plastic

Most bottles will have a security ring under the cap which will need to be removed. This can easily be cut away with a knife or scissors.

Step 3:
Cut bottle to size

Use a sharp knife to cut the threaded neck from each pair of bottles. Trim each bottle to the flange under the threaded neck. These flanges will be connected to create our container.

Step 4: Compartment separation (optional)

Follow this step only if you want to create two compartments inside the container. Cut a small circular shape from the remainder of the soda bottle, larger than the diameter of the flange of the threaded neck. This will be glued in between the flanges to make two separate waterproof compartments inside each container.

Tip:

To ensure maximum waterproofing, it is best to choose a non-water soluble adhesive for sticking your compartments together.

Step 5:
Glue flanges together

Using a strong adhesive, apply glue to the underside of both flanges and clamp together, flange to flange, and clamp until the glue is cured. If you want a compartment separator, insert the circular plastic disc cut from the side of the bottle between the flanges. Adhere the two sides together.

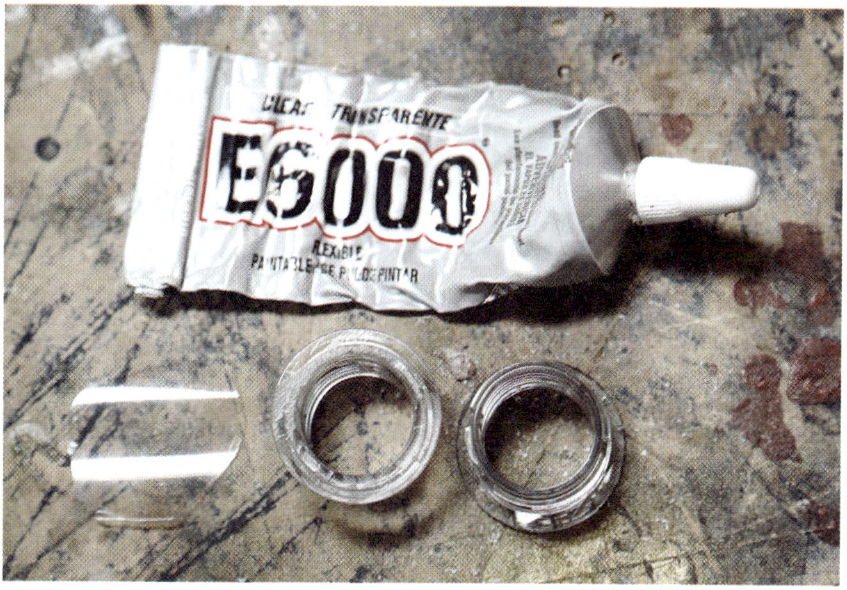

Step 6:
Labels

To keep things organized in these tiny containers, stick labels on each lid to keep your items easily identifiable.

These tiny containers are great to throw in your kit for all kinds of needs. If it's small enough to fit inside, then it's waterproof and secure. Try making these with a few different-size bottles to take all sorts of small items with you.

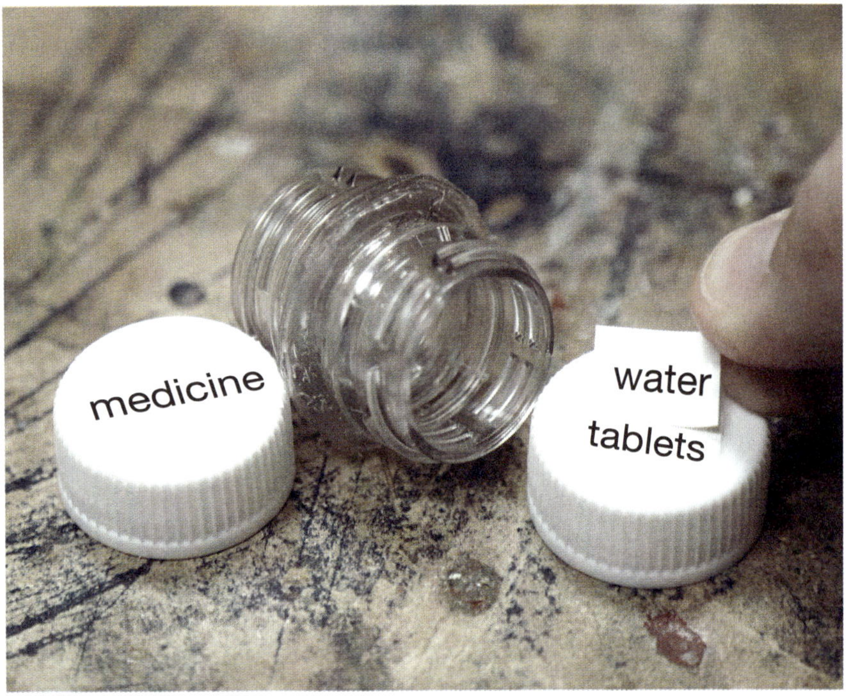

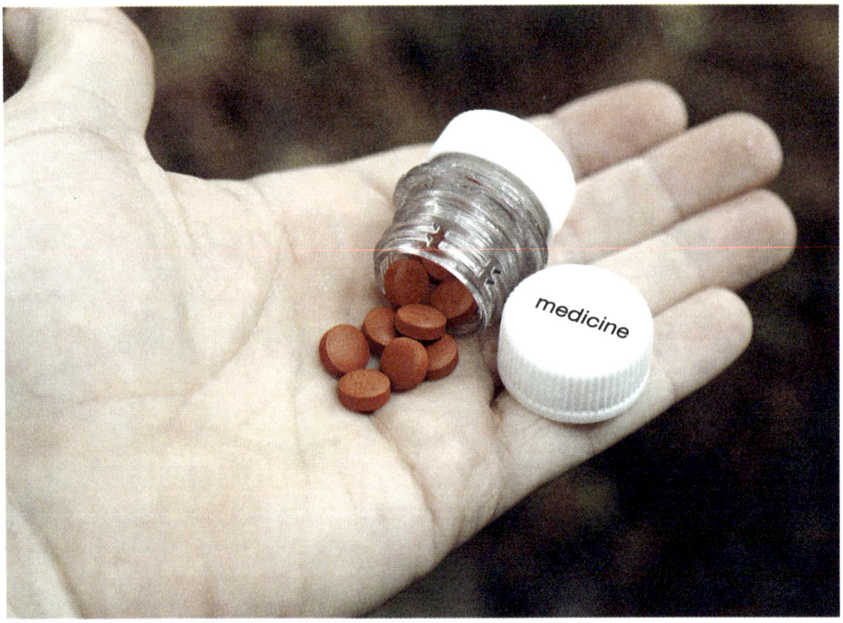

medicine

Project 09. Paracord bracelet

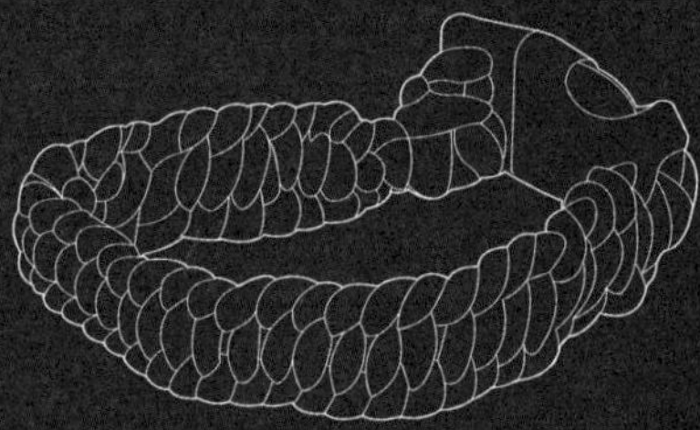

When out in the wild, few things are more versatile than paracord. It's strong and waterproof, and has a million uses. A long paracord should always be part of your gear, so why not actually carry it on you neatly braided up as a bracelet? Then it's literally always at hand when you need it. It is also a great project to make around a campfire.

Tools & Materials

Tools:

- Ruler
- Scissors/knife
- Lighter

Materials:

- Paracord at least 6 m (20 ft) or 2 × 3 m (10 ft) strands
- Plastic snap buckle

Step 1: Gather supplies

The bracelet is made from two strands of paracord that are braided together. This means you have the option of using two different colours of paracord to create your design. I chose two types of high-visibility yellow. Since paracord is synthetic, we'll use the lighter to melt the ends of the cord after cutting to prevent unravelling.

Step 2: Wrap end around wrist

Start by wrapping one end of paracord loosely around your wrist. We'll use this length of paracord to determine the circumference of your wrist.

Step 3: Measure

Find where the paracord overlaps with the end on your wrist and pinch that part of the paracord to mark the circumference, then lay the paracord down next to a ruler and measure the length of paracord needed to go around your wrist. Every 2.5 cm (1 in) of wrist length equals 30cm (12 in) of paracord needed. My wrist circumference was 20 cm (8 in), so I needed 240 cm (8 ft) of paracord.

Cut two lengths of paracord for the length you need. These two strands will be braided together to make the bracelet.

Step 4: Tie ends through buckle

Gather an end from each paracord strand and tie the end in a simple knot. This knot will be hidden under the braid, so it doesn't have to be complicated or fancy, just enough to stop the braid from unravelling.

Feed the ends of the paracord through one of the buckle loops and pull through until the knot is up against the buckle.

Step 5:
Space buckles and prepare the braid

Feed the loose ends of the paracord lengths through the other buckle loop. Using the ruler, space the buckle ends apart the same distance as the circumference of your wrist.

Lay your buckle down on a flat surface and position the strands so they run straight from one buckle to the other, and then have each strand go off to opposing sides. This will make the braid much easier to understand on your first try.

Bring one strand of paracord (in this example, the bottom one) underneath the buckles and upwards. Bring the other strand of paracord (in this example, the top one) and lay it over the first paracord strand.

Step 6: Pull tight

Gently pull on the paracord strands to close the knot without moving the buckle placement: this will secure the buckle in place.

You've just completed the first braid, and have set the stage for the same braid to be completed again and again until the space between the buckles has been covered with braids.

Tip

Once you get the technique down you can incorporate items into your bracelet, such as a watch face or a mini compass, to make your paracord bracelet even more functional.

Step 7:
Continue braid

Continue making the same braid again by passing the bottom strand under the buckle and upwards, then the other strand over the buckles and through the loop made by the first paracord strand.

Step 8:
Flatten as you go

After a few braids are completed, take the time to make sure the paracord is nice and tight along the completed braids by pulling on the paracord strands. If your bracelet is starting to twist, you may have missed a step or completed the braid backwards. If you're using two different paracord colours, this should be easy to spot and undo.

Step 9: Ending braid

Continue the braid until you reach the other buckle, making sure to end your braiding as close as possible to the buckle. You may be able to tighten up your braids and squeeze another braid or two in there.

Tie a simple overhand knot with the two paracord colours to secure the braid.

We deliberately overestimated the amount of paracord needed by a little, so trim off extra paracord with a knife or scissors, leaving a small tail from each.

Step 10: Secure and melt ends

Once the ends have been trimmed, we can melt the paracord with a lighter to prevent unravelling. Hold a lighter to the end of the paracord to ignite it and let the paracord burn for a few seconds so that it melts. Then blow out the flame and use the blunt end of the lighter to press the molten end into the knot, securing the knot and smoothing out the end in one go.

Step 11: Buckle up!

Once the melted ends have cooled, your paracord bracelet is ready for action in any survival situation. Simply unbuckle the bracelet and then work the melted ends from the knot you tied. Begin unwinding the braids to reveal your full length of paracord – in my case, 240 cm (8 ft). You now have a long length of paracord ready for deployment!

There's no reason to stop with a bracelet. You can easily store loads of paracord this way by making a tether for your water bottle or a handle for your pack, or beef up any other strap on your pack by braiding it with paracord.

Project 10. Cordage from plastic bottle

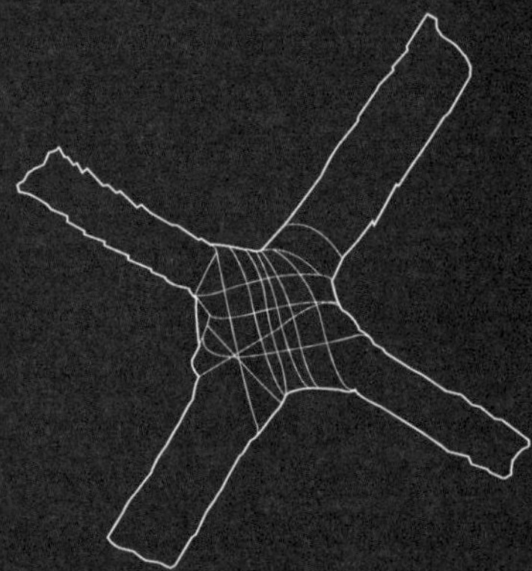

When out enjoying nature the last thing we should be doing is leaving rubbish behind – especially plastic bottles. No matter the size or type, you can easily make loads of cordage from a single bottle, which can be used for anything from lashing to securing items together.

Tools & Materials

Tools:

- Knife
- Scrap wood
- Saw

Materials:

- Plastic water or soda bottles

Tip:
Use scrap wood or found timber wherever possible to make your DIYs more sustainable and affordable – there's no need to break the bank on new materials.

Step 1: Find wood

The process to make cordage from a plastic bottle is deceptively simple. Any stick will suffice, but for clarity I will be using scrap timber to illustrate the cuts required. For best results, the wood to use to make the cordage should be at least 25 mm × 25 mm (1 in × 1 in).

Step 2:
Make cuts

Using a saw, start by making sure the end of the wood we're using is squared. We'll be making two cuts on this end of the wood.

Locate the centre of the wood and make the first cut straight through, cut to about 40 mm (1½ in) from the end. Next, rotate the wood 90 degrees away from you along the long axis and make the second cut perpendicular to the first, but only cutting halfway through the wood.

The second cut will be where the blade of our knife will rest, and the first cut will be where the bottle is fed through to create the cordage.

Step 3: Start cordage cut

Cut either end off the plastic bottle – we want to use the plastic at its thinnest part. With a straight edge of the cut plastic bottle, make a tapered incision parallel to the edge to get the cordage started (see below).

Step 4: Insert blade

Make sure your knife is sharpened before inserting the blade into the shallow slot made earlier. Insert the blade into the shallow opening and tap into place so the blade bites into the wood and is securely seated.

Step 5: Start cordage

Insert the tapered end of the cordage started earlier through the opening between the inserted knife and the cut made through the wood. The size of this opening will dictate how thick your cordage will eventually be.

Tip:
Take care that the knife doesn't dislodge as you are pulling the cordage through by applying pressure with your foot as you pull – always be very careful when using sharp knives.

Step 6: Make cordage

Gently pull on the tapered end to pull the soda bottle through the opening and make cordage. You may need to coax the bottle by turning it with your other hand to ensure a consistent width of cordage as you pull.

Step 7: Cordage usage

It is possible to make a few shallow cuts in the wood to create different width cordage. If you see that the cordage is getting too thin as you are pulling, gently ease the bottle back on track to achieve as consistent a width of cordage as possible.

The great thing about using plastic bottles for cordage is that it is surprisingly strong. There are plenty of applications where using cordage of different widths could be useful, from attaching a tarp to a tree or hanging equipment for storage.

Mini project

Milk jug lantern

Tools:

- None

Materials:

- Headband flashlight
- Any translucent container

Level up your light source by turning your headlamp into a super-bright lantern to make your campsite a little cozier. An alternative to the directional light that your headlamp casts, this kind will light up the area all around it and be seen from far away.

Step 1: Gather container

Any translucent container will do, but these 2 litre (70 fl oz) milk jugs are great. They are made of thin-walled plastic that is translucent, letting light shine through and then bounce around, causing the entire container to illuminate.

Step 2: Prepare flashlight

Make sure you have a proper headband flashlight with a stretchy band, so it will fit nice and snugly around the container. As ever when going on a trip into the wild, make sure you have fresh batteries packed.

Step 3:
Attach flashlight

Place your flashlight over the top of the container, sliding it to around halfway down. Now, flip the lamp part of the flashlight so that it is facing inwards, towards the container.

Step 4:
Adjust fit

Adjust the fit of the headband so it is secure around the container. You're now ready to switch the flashlight on and illuminate your campsite!

Project 11. Tarp Shelter

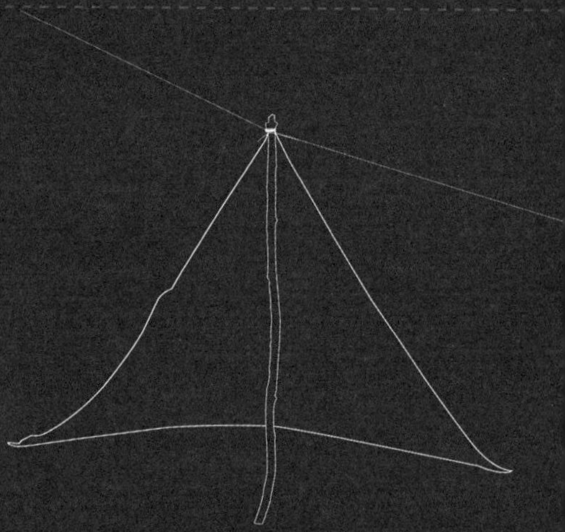

There are plenty of ways to make a complicated shelter, but when you're alone in the wilderness and need to get under cover quickly this has to be the easiest way. This shelter is dead simple, can be made with minimal supplies, and is set up in under 5 minutes.

Tools & Materials

Tools:

- Knife

Materials:

- Paracord
- Large tarpaulin
- Long, straight branch
- 3 large rocks (or any weights)
- Saw
- Shovel (optional)

Step 1: Scope location

As with all shelter, location is critical. However, in the wild, you may not always have the luxury of finding the ideal spot. The great part about this type of shelter is that you can make it work with whatever spot you happen to find, and it doesn't rely on a perfectly flat surface or need anything you couldn't reasonably find anywhere in the wilderness.

You'll need a few large rocks to hold down the corners of the tarp, and a long sturdy branch to hold up the opening.

Once you've found your spot, lay the tarp out over the area you wish to use.

Step 2:
Secure corners

With the tarp laid out, search for three large rocks to secure the corners of the tarp. If you can't find rocks, use any weights you may find in your area, like a large tree branch or, if you are near a water source, fill three containers with water.

Position the rocks or chosen weights on the corners you wish to be secured, leaving the corner with no rocks as the opening for the tarp. Be mindful of which corner will be your opening; you want to keep the opening protected from wind and weather once the shelter is constructed. Best to have the opening facing an obstruction of some kind, like a large boulder, which will protect you when you're inside.

Step 3:
Corner slack

With the tarp flat on the ground and three anchor corners identified, we need to give the corners a bit of slack for when the open corner is lifted. Gently pull each corner of the tarp towards the centre about 300 mm (12 in) with the rock anchors still on the corners.

Step 4:
Shelter pole

To make this tarp into a shelter, you need a pole to hold up the opening. Search around for any long and straight branch. The branch doesn't have to be perfectly straight, though this will help with construction and keep the entrance tidy.

The branch used should be longer than the tallest person using the shelter. Use a saw to trim down the branch as needed.

Step 5: Dig pole cavity

To prevent the pole from moving, both during construction and afterwards, a shallow cavity can be dug into the ground to help anchor the pole.

Fold back the open corner of the tarp. Using a shovel or the end of your branch dig a 150 mm (6 in) cavity into the ground where the open corner of the tarp was. The hole doesn't need to be too deep – just enough to stop the pole from being kicked out once erect.

Step 6: Position branch

Lay the branch along the tarp with one end of the branch in line with the corner of the tarp. When the branch is secured to the corner of the tarp, the branch can be lifted upwards, taking the loose corner of the tarp with it, and then the bottom of the branch can be placed into the cavity.

Step 7:
Secure tarp to branch

Using a length of paracord, tie the end of the branch to the loose corner of the tarp. Make sure to bind the two together securely so the wind doesn't pull the tarp away. It won't matter which knot you use here, as no one will see it. You just need to be able to undo the knot later when you're done using your shelter.

Step 8:
Guylines

Before erecting the branch to create the opening, you will need guylines to help stabilize the freestanding branch. For this, we'll use two lengths of paracord around the top of the branch, and then secure these to the ground to prevent the erected branch from falling over.

Step 9: Guyline knot

Double back one end of your paracord about 150 mm (6 in), then make a simple knot with the double-over length of paracord to form a simple loop. Repeat this process with another length of paracord so you have two sections of paracord with a loop on one end of each.

These tied paracord loops will slip over the top of the branch above where it is tied to the tarp. Place both loops onto the branch before erecting.

Step 10: Erect branch

With the prep work done, we're ready to lift the branch and reveal the shelter opening. Gently lift the end of the branch tied to the tarp upwards and place the end into the cavity dug earlier. The slack in the tarp should now pull tight as the branch is erected vertically. Once the branch is seated into the cavity, hold the branch with one hand and grab onto the two loose guylines with your other hand, pulling them downwards until they are taut.

You should now be able to let go of the branch and walk away from the opening while holding onto the guylines to keep the branch from tipping over. Walk the guylines outwards and find two suitable locations to secure the lines, such as a downed tree, a boulder, or tent stakes if you have them.

Step 11: Make adjustments

Chances are that the anchored corners shifted a little during construction. After the branch has been secured, gently pull on each corner to make the tarp taut, creating a spacious interior under the tarp.

Project 12. Hiking stick

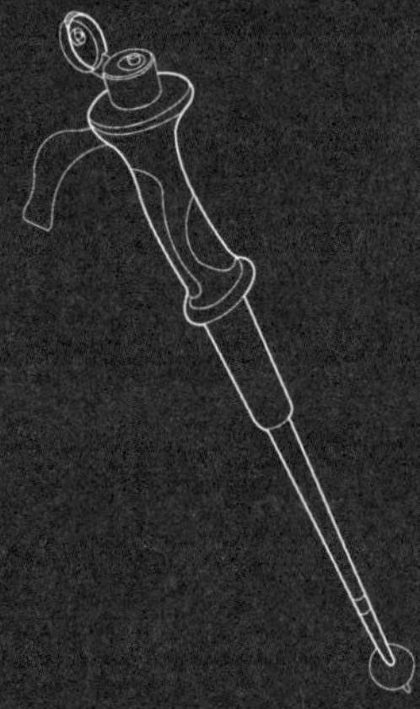

Travelling in the wilderness is thirsty work. When you want a drink around a campfire reach for your hiking stick, cleverly concealing your tipple of choice. Depending on the type of hiking pole you use, you can fit a few drams worth in each pole, enough for a few friends to join you – or maybe just enjoy a party of one.

Tools & Materials

Tools:

- Drill
- Knife

Materials:

- Aluminium hiking pole/ski pole
- Vinyl tube
- Wine cork
- Travel-size container with cap
- Glue

Step 1:
Remove pole handle

Most hiking poles have handles that can be pulled off. If yours are stubborn, try clamping down on the pole and softly tapping the underside of the handle with a mallet. Once the handle is off, you can see how much space you have in the cavity inside the pole.

Step 2:
Vinyl tube

Find a vinyl tube that fits inside your hiking poles. The vinyl tube I found also fits neatly into the travel-size container I used. For me, 16 mm (⅝ in) diameter vinyl tubing works perfectly.

Tip:
It's always a good idea to keep any leftover materials when you've finished a DIY project. Save any excess vinyl tubing and it's bound to come in handy on another make.

Step 3: Cut tube to length

With the handle off the pole, feed the tube into the pole to see how much can fit inside. Pull out and cut the vinyl tube to length, adding a little extra into your length which will be trimmed down later.

Step 4:
Measure opening for handle

Drill an opening at the top of the pole handle for the travel container top. Measure the diameter of the container top you are using and find a drill bit diameter that matches as close as possible to that diameter. I used a 19 mm (¾ in) spade bit.

Step 5: Drill opening in handle

With the handle secured in a vice, centre the drill in the handle top and drill an opening. This opening will be aligned with the channel inside the handle where the pole is inserted.

Step 6: Plug tube with cork

To prevent any liquids from leaking out the bottom of the vinyl tube, a plug is needed. The quick method is to double over the end and close it with a zip tie, but that can mean the pinched tube gets wider and may not fit as neatly inside the pole. A better method is to use a slightly oversized cork in the bottom, which is held firmly in place and waterproof to prevent leaking.

Using a sharp knife, cut a section off from a wine cork and shave it into a tapered cylinder. Insert this into the vinyl tube, then seal the end with strong adhesive to prevent the cork slipping out. Make sure the cork has complete contact with the vinyl tubing so that no liquids make contact with the adhesive directly.

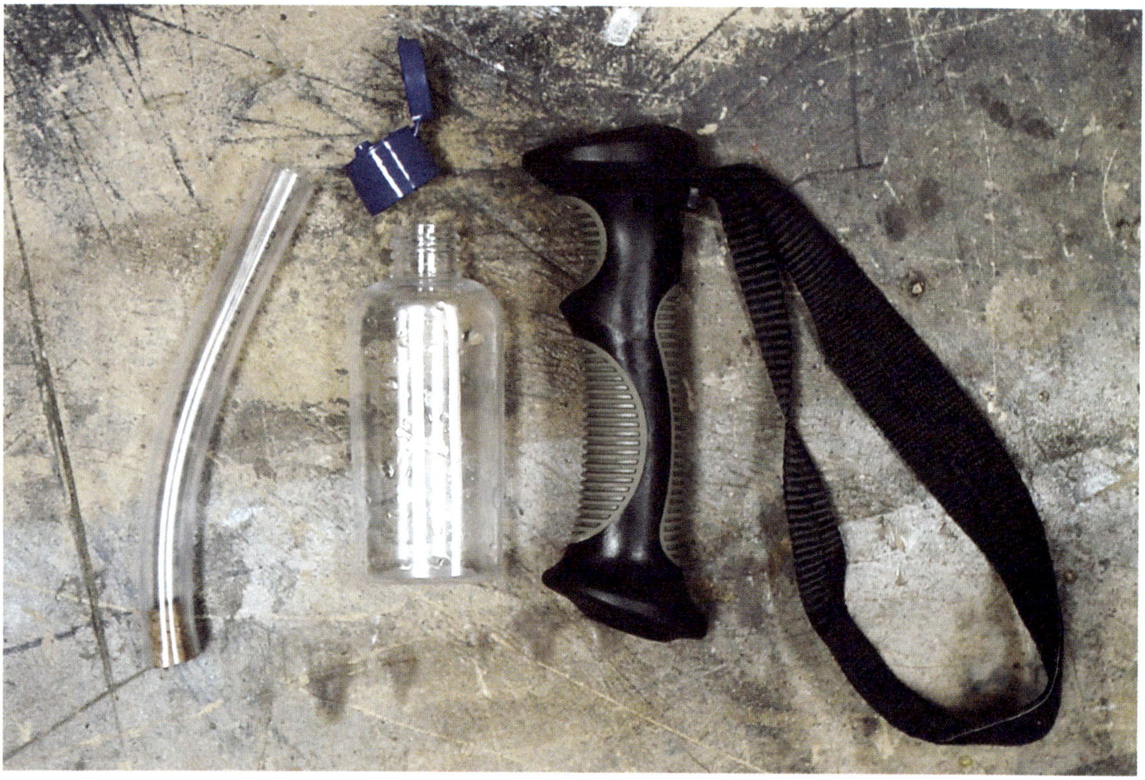

Step 7:
Cut travel bottle

Remove the cap from the travel bottle by making an initial cut on the bottle at the shoulder, then trimming up the remainder so that just the cap of the bottle is left.

Step 8: Combine vinyl tube and container top

Insert the vinyl tube into the container top. You want a very tight fit, but use no adhesives. If your tube is undersized, you can increase its diameter by wrapping tape around the tube in successive layers until reaching the diameter required.

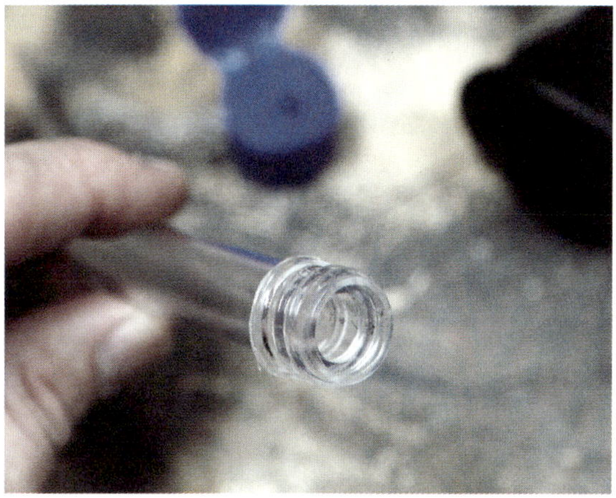

Step 9: Insert tube and top assembly into handle

Insert the vinyl tube and container top into the handle through the opening. You can secure the underside of the container top to the handle with strong adhesive, as no liquids or human contact will be made at this location.

Step 10: Place handle back on pole

Feed the vinyl tube back into the pole, put the handle back onto the hiking pole and push it back into place. To ensure a snug fit, try twisting the handle back and forth as you place it back onto the pole.

Step 11: Fill and cap

All that's left is to fill your hiking pole up with your favourite beverage and then set out on the trail.

Project 13. Folding camp stool

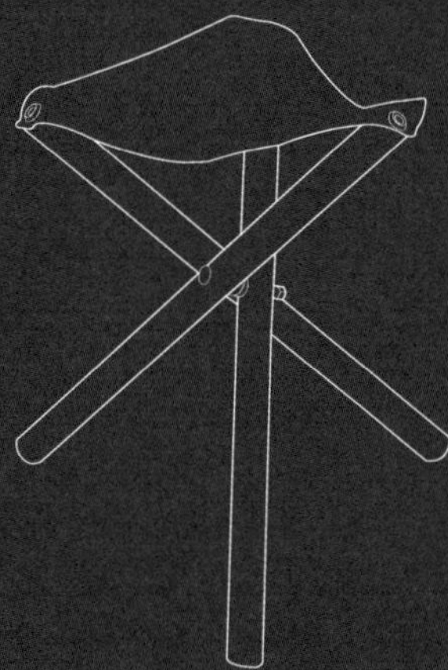

Having things take up less space is the key to taking all the stuff you'll need camping, and maybe allowing you the room to take a luxury item like this custom camp stool too. With a minimal design and a collapsing frame, these small camp stools can be made for a fraction of shop-bought ones.

Tools & Materials

Tools:

- Wood saw
- Sandpaper, 120 grit
- Knife
- Drill (with bit + driver)
- Chalk or pencil
- Screwdriver
- 2× Wrenches
- Ruler/tape measure

Materials:

- Wood dowel 2 m (6 ft) long at least 74mm (1½ in) in diameter
- 1× Carriage bolt 8 mm (5⁄16 in) with 2 nuts
- 2× Flat washers
- 1× Eye bolt 8 mm (5⁄16 in) with 2 nuts
- Leather hide (at least 2 mm thick)
- 3× Short screws
- 3× Finishing washers

Step 1:
Measure leg dowels

Your height will determine how long you want the stool legs to be, but for most adults a stool height of 60 cm (2 ft) will be perfect. Use a ruler to measure your dowel and divide into 3 equal lengths, which will be used for the stool's legs.

Step 2: Make cuts

Secure the dowel and make cuts at your indicated marks with a wood saw. I used a finishing saw, which has finer teeth than a construction saw, which has fewer and larger teeth to quickly cut wood.

Step 3: Clean ends

After cutting the dowels to length, the ends will be rough and require smoothing. Smoothing over the edges will also give your stool an eased edge, which will help the leather seat distribute weight more efficiently.

Use 120 grit sandpaper to remove the rough edge of the cut dowels and give a nice smooth radius.

Step 4: Find pivot point

There's a point on the dowel legs which will be the pivot point where the legs move together for storage and then splay out for seating. This point is offset from the midpoint of the dowel leg length, about 50 mm (2 in).

Use a tape-measure to find the midpoint of your dowel leg and make a mark. Then measure 50 mm (2 in) from the midpoint and mark. This second mark is where a hole will be drilled.

Mark the other 2 legs in the same fashion.

Step 5:
Drill openings

To give the bolt a little wiggle room, I chose a drill bit that was slightly larger than the bolt I was using. I used a 9.5 mm (⅜ in) drill bit to drill straight through each dowel at the pivot point marked.

Step 6:
Hardware

Push the carriage bolt through the hole on one of the legs, then put on a washer, the eye bolt, and another washer. Finish by adding another dowel and attach both nuts.

Step 7:
Double up nuts

By using two nuts, we can lock the nuts together and prevent them from loosening. Tighten the inside nut snug up the hardware, ensuring that the hardware is tight enough that it doesn't jiggle around. Now twist on the second nut until it meets the first. Using two wrenches, twist the nuts in opposite directions, locking them into each other.

Step 8: Last leg

Push the threaded end of the eye bolt out from in-between the two fastened dowels and put the eye bolt through the last dowel leg.

Step 9: Seat anchor points

With the legs attached together, we can turn to the seat. From where the hardware attachments are placed on the leg, the longer length will be the legs that touch the ground and the shorter length will be for the seat.

Collapse the stool flat and ensure all the legs are the same orientation. Drill a pilot hole in the centre on the "short" side of the dowels. This will be the anchor point for the leather seat.

Step 10: Cut seat

Open the seat up and place the short side ends on your piece of leather. You should be able to draw a triangle between each leg with a 25 mm (1 in) outside offset where the legs touch the leather. Make this outline with chalk or pencil.

With sharp scissors, cut the outline from your hide. Make a small hole at the seat connection points in the leather. We'll use this as our screw opening when we attach the seat to the dowels.

Step 11:

Leather reinforcement

Even with the edge of the dowels sanded with a radius, it will help to add a second small scrap of leather as reinforcement here. There is a lot of strain pulling at the anchor points from the weight of sitting, so adding this reinforcement will help ease the leather over the dowel edge.

Cut a scrap of thick leather (or double up thinner leather) and make a small hole for the screw.

Step 12:

Screw down anchor

Line up the reinforcement leather with the seat leather openings, then place a finishing washer on a screw, and screw through both leather openings and into the pilot hole on the end of the dowel. Do not tighten.

Repeat this process for the other two legs, not tightening any of the screws. Position the stool with the legs fully opened and set your leather and reinforcements into their final positions. Using a hand screwdriver, tighten each screw partially to prevent the leather from twisting around any one screw, and to ensure the legs maintain their equidistance.

Step 13:
Add a strap

If you have some extra leather scraps, you can make a carrying strap from one of the seat anchors and attach it to the pivot hardware.

These camping stools don't take up much space but are stylish and functional around the campfire or in the woods.

Project 14. Wristwatch survival

You might be surprised at the wealth of survival wonder that's inside your wristwatch. Though this project focuses on an analogue version of the watch, there is overlap with digital watches you may find useful. If you're feeling extra inspired you could replace the wristband with paracord (p82), doubling its usefulness.

Tools & Materials

Tools:

- Knife
- Scissors
- Pen
- Straight edge

Materials:

- Wristwatch

Step 1: Open

Most watches will have a removable back which allows you to replace the battery. There is typically some kind of indent along the back with a visual marking to indicate where to pry open. This watch has a small triangle engraved on the flat back where an indent is located. Using the blade of your knife, carefully insert the point into the indent and twist to pry open the watch.

Be careful here, as the watch back is fitted very tightly.

Step 2: Parts

With the back off the watch we can remove the rest of the parts. Most analogue watches will have one or more side buttons which attach to the body of the watch inside the casing. These pins will need to be removed in order to release the inside watch body and face. Either back the pins out with the tip of your knife, or just break the pins and remove the watch innards. The glass front of the watch is also pressure fit in place and can be carefully knocked out of the metal housing with a blunt stick, or a rock wrapped in cloth.

Once apart, you'll have the watch casing, the watch back, the wrist straps, the watch insides with clock face, and the glass watch front. We'll use these elements in different ways to make survival implements. Maybe you can brainstorm a few new ideas too.

Step 3: Reflector

The back of the watch can be used it as a reflector in the daytime. The inside of the watch back will be shiny and is very good at reflecting sunlight, perfect for getting attention when in the wild. Even painted or coloured watches will have a shiny inside. And, unlike a mirror, this watch back can't shatter and break.

Practise directing sunlight to somewhere nearby first to become familiar with your reflecting technique.

When you're ready, you can easily signal people very far away by flashing the reflector towards them to get their attention. If you're feeling confident, you can try to flash out Morse code and send a message!

Step 4: Sundial

It may seem strange to make a sundial from a watch; however, in a survival situation where your watch is dead this will come in handy.

There is a reason that you still see sundials around today – they were carefully designed and can tell time accurately. The sun casts a shadow on the dial plate when it strikes the lifted arm that extends from the centre of the dial plate; the narrow arm of the shadow falls on time increments on the dial face, and will change as the shadow moves throughout the day.

Since the sun's shadow will be different at the equator than they are further towards the poles, the sundial arm will also need to vary in length in order to obtain an accurate reading. The angle that the arm is set at is called the gnomon. To tell correct time, the gnomon needs to be parallel with the earth's axis and should point towards true north.

Consult a map and determine your approximate latitude, ideally before you're in dire need of knowing (like before you leave for your hike or camping trip). This latitude is what your gnomon should be set at. Approximate is fine, since we're only interested in rough passage of time, not precise timekeeping.

Most of the world's population lives in the latitudes of 30° south to 60° north, with 0° being the equator. Drawing latitude bands around a globe, that means 0°-30° south is roughly Australia, South Africa and Brazil. 0°-30° north is North Africa, Southeast Asia, and Central America. 30°-60° north is North America, Europe and Asia.

Imagining we were hiking in France, we could approximate the latitude as 50°, therefore the gnomon of our sundial would also be 50°.

Try to align your sundial when the sun is at its highest above you and use that to set your sundial at 12 o'clock. Knowing the sun moves westwards about 15° an hour, you can start refining the watch dial to tell time more accurately and eventually be able to use the minute ticks on the watch face to tell time with greater accuracy.

Step 5: Remove glass front

The glass front from most wristwatches is fit into place with friction and uses the watch face to keep it in place. A gentle blow from a blunt stick on the front of the glass should dislodge it from the watch casing.

Step 6:

Salvage leather

If you didn't upgrade the strap of your watch to a paracord strap (p82) then we can use the leather for strapping. Remove the watch straps from the watch casing, reserving the integrity of the leather as much as possible.

If your leather is bonded, gently pry the leather straps apart to reveal the laminated layers. Though all the material is useful, we are particularly interested in the leather parts of the strap.

Step 7:

Slice leather into strip

Using a pen, or any other sharp implement, mark a serpentine path on the leather strap, making the longest leather strip possible from each piece of leather. Use a knife or scissors to cut the leather along the marked lines and create the continuous thin strip of leather strapping.

Step 8: Glass blade

We won't be able to make a big knife from such a small watch, but we can make a small sharp blade from a fragment of glass from the watch face. To start, place the glass watch front into a large leaf and fold the leaf completely around the glass. Place the glass-wrapped leaf onto a sturdy surface like a flat rock or root, and then strike with a large rock to break the glass.

Try to aim at the edge of the glass, thereby ensuring larger fragments, whereas a direct centre hit would shatter the glass into tiny pieces. We want large glass fragments.

Step 9:

Blade handle

We won't need a very large handle for our small glass blade but will need some kind of holder in order to handle the blade safely. Look for straight and strong sticks that aren't split at the ends, those pictured are good candidates for our blade handles.

Gently tap your knife blade into the end of one of your stick handles to create a slit. The slit should be about as deep as the blade is long.

Step 10: Blade wrapping

To hold the blade in the handle we'll need to bind the top of the handle and secure the blade in place. Start by placing one end of the leather strapping into the bottom of the slit made in the end of the handle. Carefully insert the glass blade into the slit and on top of the leather strapping end. The top of the blade should be sitting above the top of the handle.

Squeeze the sides of the handle over the blade and bind the leather strapping around the top of the handle tightly, securing the blade in the handle. The final two wraps of the strapping should be knotted to secure the binding.

This blade is great for scoring or marking, and even making cuts in thinner materials like twine and packaging.

Step 11: Housing ring

The metal carcass leftover once all the other materials from the wristwatch have been used actually has a use, too. Adding in the watch frame along your paracord tent guy wires and clotheslines gives you a great spot to anchor more lines, or redirect a paracord through.

The ring of the watch body can have items tied or hung from it – there really is a lot of utility to be had from an old watch body. Hopefully these wristwatch ideas will get you thinking of some new ways to use your own in a survival scenario.

Stay safe
Be careful when handling the broken watchface, and conserve the rest of the fragments in a wrap of paper in case you lose your 'blade' or need to make an additional knife for yourself or a buddy.

Project 15. PVC bow

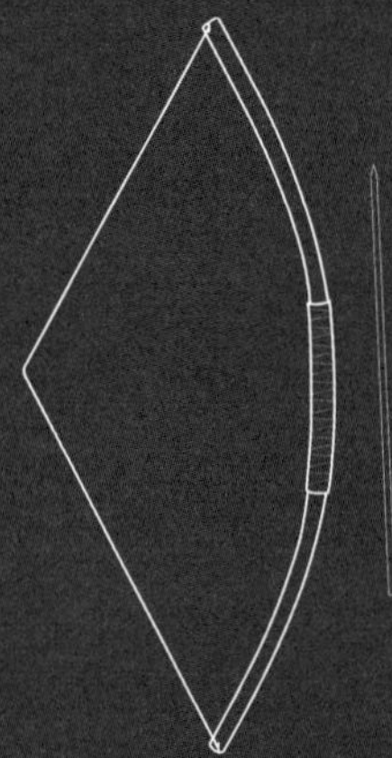

There are many ways to make a bow for a fun target-practice activity, to raise ropes into trees, or even for hunting, and it can be as simple as a piece of string on a stick. However, this PVC bow has some distinct advantages over a stick bow. It's waterproof, less likely to snap from fatigue, lightweight, and can be customized to any shape variant you like.

Tools & Materials

Tools:

- Knife
- Fine blade saw
- Lighter
- Sandpaper
- Hammer
- Marker pen

Materials:

- 30 cm (12 in) of 25 mm (1 in) PVC pipe
- 1.2 m (4 ft) of 19 mm (¾ in) PVC pipe
- 20 cm (8 in) of 13 mm (½ in) PVC pipe
- Electrical tape
- Paracord

Step 1: PVC pipe

As a practical tool, the bow is among the most important for survival. The parts of this bow are just as useful as the tool itself: the paracord string can be removed and reused in any number of ways, from a snare to guy wire, and the PVC can be used as a tent pole, fishing rod or clothes hanger. This PVC variant of a primitive tool may just be your new best friend when you're in the wilderness.

The PVC I'm using for this project is all Schedule 40. Pipe schedule is a non-dimensional number that relates to the thickness of the wall and affects the inside diameter. Schedule 40 is by far the most common type of PVC pipe used. Though Schedule 40 may have started as an American term to standardize pipes, it is widely used in other markets around the world. At your local hardware shop the plumbing department should have no trouble understanding the term.

The 19 mm (¾ in) diameter pipe will be the body of the bow. The 25 mm (1 in) diameter pipe will be slipped over the body and centred to be the handle of the bow, and the 13 mm (½ in) diameter pipe will be inserted into the ends of the body to stiffen the ends for the bow string.

Step 2: Cut 13 mm (½ in) pipe lengthways

Secure the PVC pipe to a sturdy work surface and cut along the pipe lengthways, only cutting through one wall, not all the way through. Using a saw with a fine blade, gently start at one end of the pipe and work your way along the length of the pipe.

Step 3:
Cut 13 mm (½ in) pipe in half

Once the pipe has been cut lengthways down one side, we can cut it in two. The pieces should be roughly the same length, but accuracy here isn't important. These two sections of pipe will be inserted into the bow body a little later after all the cutting has been completed.

Step 4:
Cut 25 mm (1 in) pipe lengthways

Secure the 25 mm (1 in) pipe to a workbench or sturdy surface and cut along the pipe lengthways, as before. We want to cut this pipe down one side, not all the way through. As with the smaller pipe, start at one end and carefully work your way down the pipe, cutting a slit the entire length.

Step 5: Line up pipes

The cutting is complete. You should have a long section of 19 mm (¾ in) PVC pipe, which is the body of the bow, a short section of 25 mm (1 in) PVC pipe with a slit down the length, which will be the bow handle, and two smaller 13 mm (½ in) PVC pipe sections with slits down one side that will be the reinforcement for the bow body ends.

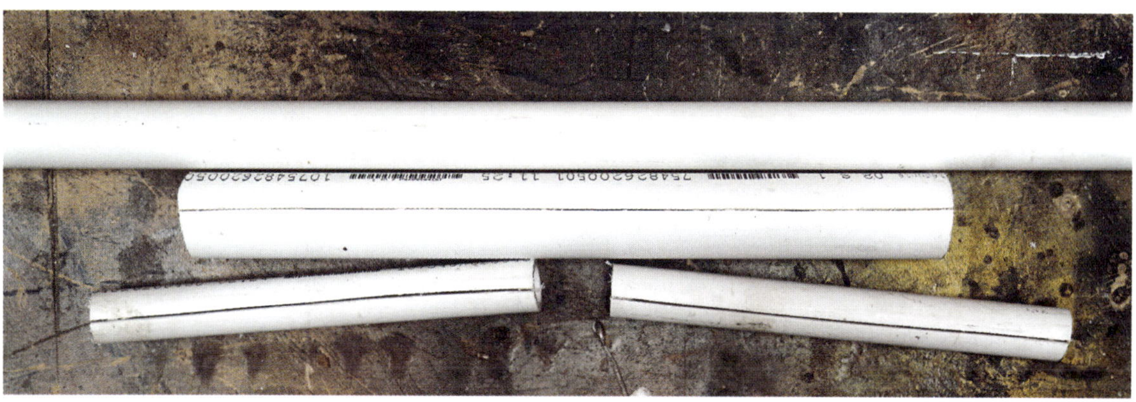

Step 6: Smoothing PVC edges

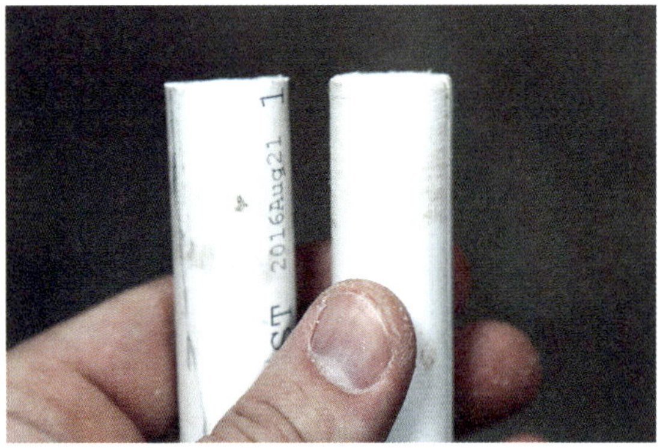

The PVC pipes can nest inside each other, but the fit is very tight, which is why we've cut a slit into some of the pieces. By removing some material we've made it easier for the pipe to stretch or compress to fit in or around the other pieces.

To help the PVC pipe we can use sandpaper to remove the sharp edges at the cut ends of the pipe. I used 80 grit sandpaper to remove the edge of the 13 mm (½ in) PVC pipe sections; this will allow them to be inserted into the 19 mm (¾ in) pipe ends a lot more easily.

Step 7: Insert pipe into bow ends

Work the 13 mm (½ in) pipe into the 19 mm (¾ in) pipe end. The fit will be tight, even with a slit cut into the smaller pipe allowing it to compress down. The hardest part is starting the insertion, but once that's in you can use a hammer to gently tap the PVC pipe into place. Continue with hammer blows until the smaller pipe is inside the larger one. It won't go all the way in, as the friction will stop the pipe from being inserted any further, but we only need about 25–50 mm (1–2 in).

With the PVC pipe inserted into one end, you can repeat the process on the other end of the bow body.

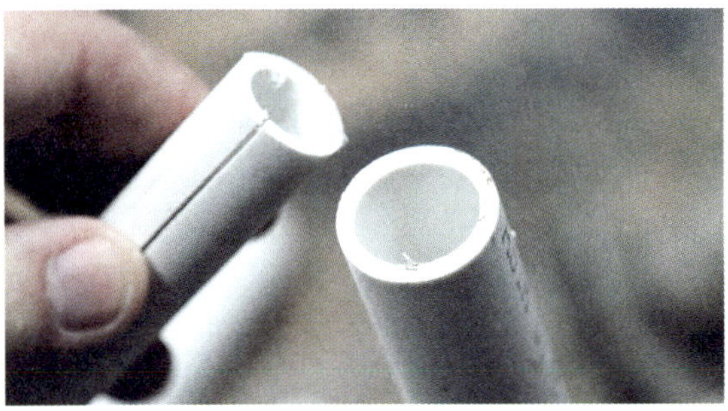

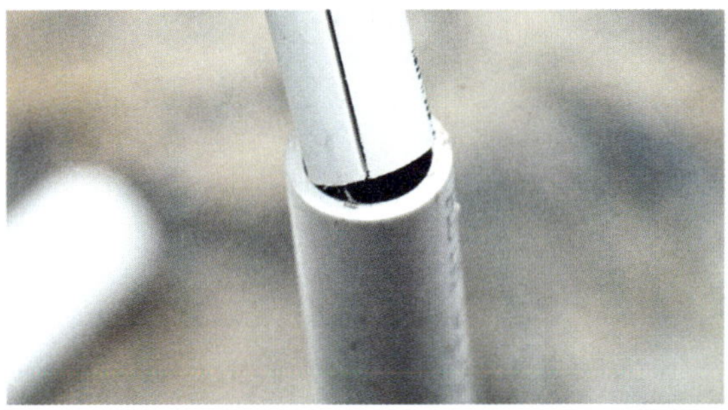

Step 8: Trim bow ends

With both ends of the bow reinforced with more PVC, we can trim up the ends from the PVC that couldn't be hammered in all the way. Use a saw to trim up both ends of the PVC bow.

Step 9: PVC handle

The 25 mm (1 in) PVC pipe handle can now be slid over the 19 mm (¾ in) PVC pipe bow body.

Use the blade of a knife to pry open the slit of the 25 mm (1 in) PVC pipe, then slip the 19 mm (¾ in) PVC pipe inside the larger pipe. Once the larger pipe has started covering the smaller one, stand the pipes upright and pound the PVC with a hammer and on the ground to force the larger pipe along the body of the smaller pipe. You can also use a hammer with some precision blows to move the pipe if it's stubborn.

The goal is to have the 25 mm (1 in) PVC pipe centred on the 19 mm (¾ in) PVC pipe bow body.

Step 10: Wrap handle

Though it might seem like friction alone could hold the PVC handle onto the PVC body, over time the handle can move and will need to be secured in place. To achieve this we'll use electrical tape to tighten the handle to the body.

Begin at the top of the handle and wrap in overlapping rounds around the handle until you reach the bottom of the handle.

Step 11:
Finding the bow front

Up to now, it isn't obvious which is the front of the bow and which is the back. Now that the handle has been secured in place we can clearly see the cut line in the handle underneath the electrical tape.

The cut line in the handle will be the front of the bow, the part that faces towards the target. You can make a mark in the PVC body with a marker if it makes things clearer.

Step 12:
Mark bow string notches

With the front of the bow established we can turn attention to the notches that will hold the bow string. These notches, at the end of the PVC bow body, need to be at right angles to the front of the bow and have a slight taper. This taper should be angled towards the back of the bow (away from the front). These notches will keep the bow string in place when the bow is drawn, so it is important to have them facing in the right direction.

Mark a bow string notch with a marker on each end of the bow body. The notches should be about 25 mm (1 in) in length and fully within the double PVC pipe on each end.

Step 13:
Cut bow string notches

Use a saw to cut the marked notches, ensuring that the cuts stay within the double PVC pipes on each end so the string tension doesn't break the PVC when under load.

Step 14:
Paracord bow string

To make the paracord bow string, take one end of the paracord and double up about 50 mm (2 in) from the end, then tie the doubled-over section in an overhand knot. This will create a loop at the end that is very secure. Make sure the cut end of the paracord is sealed with a flame to prevent the paracord from fraying.

Step 15:
Loop bow string to bow

Loop the tied end of the paracord into the notch cut into one end of the bow body and ensure it's fully seated in the notch.

Step 16: Pull string taut

With one end of the paracord bow string secured, pull it taut along the length of the bow body until you reach the other notched end. Tie a second overhand knot with doubled-over paracord about 50-75mm (2-3in) from the end of the bow body. We're deliberately tying the knot short here as the bow will flex and stretch out the paracord and we need the initial bow string to be as tight as possible.

Once tied, bend the bow body slightly and insert the loop of the paracord string through the notch to complete the bow.

Step 17: Flame paracord ends

Trim up the bow string ends as needed and ensure to seal each end with a flame to prevent the paracord from fraying. Your bow is ready to use with some simple tapered wooden arrows!

AWESOME

Golden Rules

Staying safe anytime you are out in the wild is critical. That means safety before you leave by letting someone know where you are going, safety on the trail or campsite, and safety when you go home by packing out what you brought in and letting loved ones know you're back. Every decision and action should be run through the safety-check filter. This is because if anything happens while you are in the wilderness, you're on your own, and you need to be prepared to take care of yourself. Follow these golden rules to ensure that your time in the wilderness is safe and fun.

#01

It's always better to overprepare

When preparing for an adventure, I like to keep the mindset that things will take longer than anticipated and there will be fewer resources than I expect. This isn't a defeatist attitude; it's a way of thinking that ensures I am overly prepared and mentally ready to tackle the plan for my adventure.

#02

Bring everything you need rather than expecting to find it

When in the wilderness I expect to find no shelters, no toilets, or any other conveniences. This may or may not be true, but going in with that mindset allows me to plan ahead for what I will need. In this modern world it's easy to forget that mobile phones may not work wherever you are going, and you shouldn't expect them to. It's always a good idea to travel with a printed map rather than relying on your phone.

#03

Wayfinding is a priority

Even established trails can get washed out, or you could get turned around and lost. A printed map and a compass have been a mainstay in camping packs for generations for a reason: they are simple, and they work. Carry both with you. Along with knowing where you are going, it's important to be honest about your abilities and have reasonable expectations on how far you expect to travel. Pay attention to elevation gains, as a short path on a map can be deceptive and require more effort than you think.

#04

Your mother was right when she said to bring a sweater

Weather can change quickly when you're out exploring, and having layers of clothing helps regulate your body temperature and keep you comfortable. Luckily there are endless options for compact waterproof jackets and trousers. Invest in some decent gear: you'll be thankful for your foresight when you need it.

#05

Leave nothing behind

Lastly, the golden rule any time you're out in the wild is to **leave nature in a better state than you found it**. Not only does that mean pack out what you brought in, but if you see some rubbish at a campsite then pick it up. The beauty and pristine forests and trails of nature only stay that way if we all contribute.

What you'll need in the wild

Any experienced camper will have a few essentials they take with them anywhere they go. For those of you who are makers and campers, there are a few more items you may want to add to your kit, making you the master maker in and out of the workshop.

Besides your well-worn camping knife and seasoned cast-iron pan, here are a few more maker-centric essentials you'll need in the wild:

- Multitool
- Hot glue stick
- Neodymium magnet
- Hacksaw
- Stiff wire
- Candles
- Radio
- Waterproof adhesive (such as E6000)
- Extra pair of socks (trust me!)

Resources

All the tools and materials used throughout the book are readily available in most DIY and hardware stores, or online. Here's a short list of places they can be found.

Screwfix (www.screwfix.com)

Toolstation (www.toolstation.com)

Wickes (www.wickes.co.uk)

Camping and outdoor equipment

Mountain Warehouse (www.mountainwarehouse.com)

Blacks (www.blacks.co.uk)

GO Outdoors (www.gooutdoors.co.uk)

Arthur Beale (www.arthurbeale.co.uk)

Index

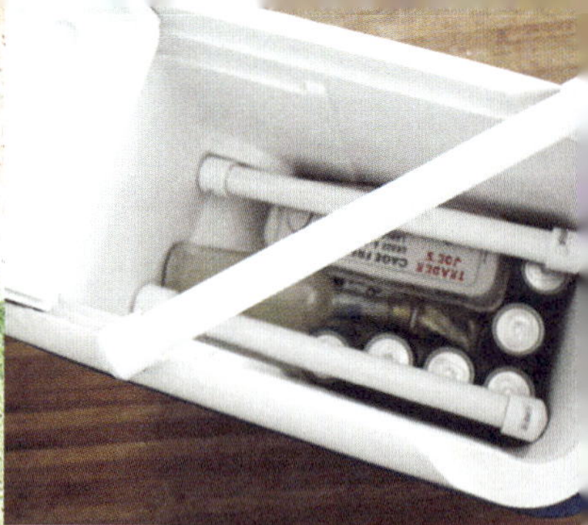

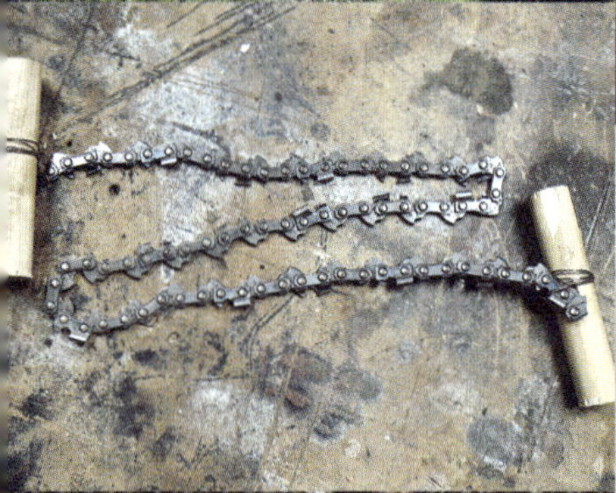
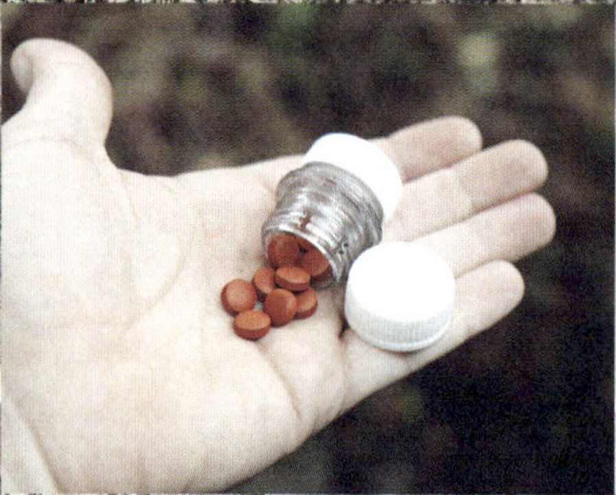

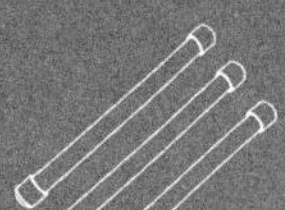

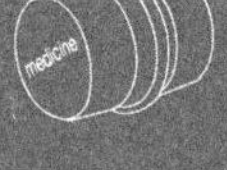
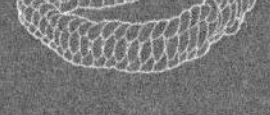